W9-AGG-142

Growing Up with SCIENCE®

Third Edition

13

Semiconductor–Sports science

Marshall Cavendish
Reference
New York

Marshall Cavendish
99 White Plains Road
Tarrytown, NY 10591

www.marshallcavendish.us

© 2006 Marshall Cavendish Corporation
© 1987, 1990 Marshall Cavendish Limited

Library of Congress Cataloging-in-Publication Data

Growing up with science.— 3rd ed.
    p. cm.
  Includes index.
  Contents: v. 1. Abrasive-Astronomy — v. 2. Atmosphere-Cable television —
v. 3. Cable travel-Cotton — v. 4. Crane-Electricity — v. 5 Electric motor-
Friction — v. 6. Fuel cell-Immune system — v. 7. Induction-Magnetism —
v. 8. Mapmaking-Mining and quarrying — v. 9. Missile and torpedo-Oil
exploration and refining — v. 10. Optics-Plant kingdom — v. 11. Plasma
physics-Radiotherapy — v. 12. Railroad system-Seismology — v. 13.
Semiconductor-Sports — v. 14. Spring-Thermography — v. 15. Thermometer-
Virus, biological — v. 16. Virus, computer-Zoology — v. 17. Index.
  ISBN 0-7614-7505-2 (set)
  ISBN 0-7614-7518-4 (vol. 13)
  1. Science—Encyclopedias.

Q121.G764 2006
503—dc22

                                                              2004049962
                                           09 08 07 06 05 6 5 4 3 2 1

Printed in China

CONSULTANT

Donald R. Franceschetti, Ph.D.
Dunavant Professor at the University of Memphis

Donald R. Franceschetti is a member of the American
Chemical Society, the American Physical Society, the
Cognitive Science Society, the History of Science Society,
and the Society for Neuroscience.

CONTRIBUTORS TO VOLUME 13
Chris Cooper
Tom Jackson
Freddy Tipple

Marshall Cavendish
Editors: Peter Mavrikis and Susan Rescigno
Editorial Director: Paul Bernabeo
Production Manager: Alan Tsai

The Brown Reference Group
Editors: Leon Gray and Simon Hall
Designer: Sarah Williams
Picture Researchers: Susy Forbes and Laila Torsun
Indexer: Kay Ollerenshaw
Illustrators: Darren Awuah and Mark Walker
Managing Editor: Bridget Giles
Art Director: Dave Goodman

CONTENTS

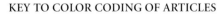

KEY TO COLOR CODING OF ARTICLES

■ EARTH, SPACE, AND ENVIRONMENTAL SCIENCES

■ LIFE SCIENCES AND MEDICINE

■ MATHEMATICS

■ PHYSICS AND CHEMISTRY

■ TECHNOLOGY

■ PEOPLE

Semiconductor

Semiconductors are materials that can conduct an electrical current, though not as well as metals. The development of semiconductor materials started the present revolution in electronics. They make possible many different types of electrical devices, such as computers, solar cells, telephones, and televisions.

Among the most common semiconductors are chemical elements that are not quite metals yet not quite nonmetals either. Scientists call these elements metalloids, and they include antimony, arsenic, boron, germanium, selenium, and silicon. Of these, by far the most important elements for use as semiconducting materials are germanium and silicon. Silicon is the basis of the silicon chip, microprocessor, and solar cell.

A number of compounds also behave as semiconductors. Many are intermetallic compounds, which are a mixture of two metallic elements. Among the most useful are gallium arsenide (GaAs) and indium antimonide (InSb). Glass and even certain plastics (such as polyvinyl chloride; PVC) can also sometimes act as semiconductors.

Semiconductor action

In a pure semiconductor, for example, pure silicon, one silicon atom forms bonds with other silicon atoms by sharing electrons in its outer electron shell. In this way, each silicon atom gains a full complement of eight electrons in the outer electron shell, forming a stable structure. However, a few of these electrons can escape from their bonds, leaving holes behind. Other electrons can move into the holes. If electricity is applied to the silicon, a tiny electrical current will flow. The negatively charged electrons will travel in one direction, and the holes appear to move in the opposite direction, acting

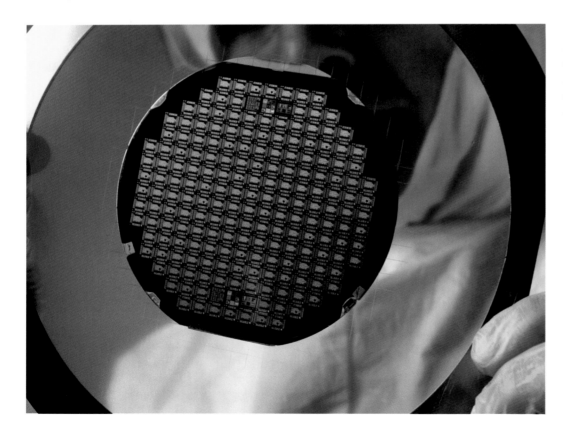

◄ *This silicon wafer has been cut from a block of pure silicon. It will be used to manufacture an integrated circuit or a microprocessor.*

STRUCTURES OF SEMICONDUCTOR CRYSTALS

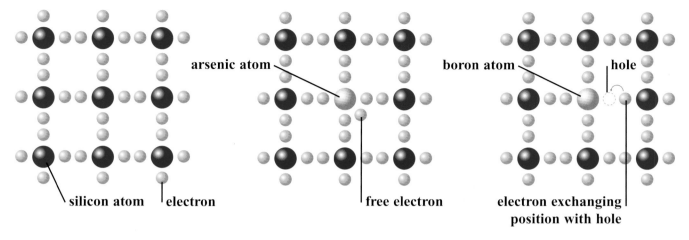

pure silicon   **n-type semiconductor**   **p-type semiconductor**

like moving positive charges. In this arrangement, the electrons are termed negative (*n*) carriers, and the holes are called positive (*p*) carriers.

In a pure semiconductor, there are not enough carriers to give the material a useful amount of conducting power. To bring it to a useful level, certain impurities must be added to the pure material. This process is called doping, and the impurities added are called dopants.

Adding dopants to the pure semiconductor raises the conductivity of the material by adding either extra electrons (*n* carriers) or extra holes (*p* carriers). The material then becomes known as either an *n*-type or *p*-type semiconductor.

Semiconductor junctions

The key to understanding the way in which semiconductors work lies in looking at what happens where the two types of semiconductor material come together. This region is called a junction. When electricity from a battery is applied to the junction between an *n*-type or *p*-type semiconductor, one of two things can happen, depending on which battery terminal is connected to which type of semiconductor.

When the positive terminal of the battery is connected to the *n*-type semiconductor, and the negative terminal is connected to the *p*-type semiconductor, the extra electrons in the *n* region tend to flow to the positive terminal, and the excess

▲ *If a silicon crystal is doped with arsenic, an extra electron in the outer shell of the arsenic atom is not involved with chemical bonding and can move around. This arrangement is called an n-type semiconductor. If the silicon is doped with boron, "holes" appear in the pattern of chemical bonds. Electrons from neighboring bonds can fill these holes, in effect allowing the holes to move as if they carried a positive charge. This arrangement is called a p-type semiconductor.*

reverse-biased configuration   **forward-biased configuration**

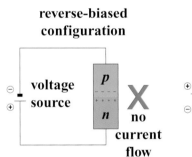
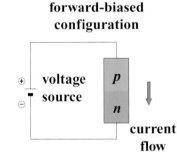

▲ *In a pn-junction diode, electrons neighboring the junction diffuse from the n-type to the p-type semiconductor, creating an electrical potential difference that resists further diffusion. If a battery is connected with the negative terminal at the p side, the electrical potential difference is further increased, and no current can flow through the diode.*

▲ *If the battery is connected with the positive terminal at the p side of the diode, the external voltage opposes the potential difference at the pn junction. If the battery voltage is large enough, it can overcome the potential difference at the junction, and current may flow through the diode.*

▶ *An npn bipolar transistor consists of a thin layer of p-type semiconductor (the base) sandwiched between two layers of n-type semiconductor (the collector and the emitter). When the electrons are removed from the base by the application of a small voltage, electrons in the emitter jump across the boundary to replace them. Some electrons diffuse through the base to the collector, allowing a current to flow around the large voltage circuit. The transistor can therefore be used as a switch, allowing current to flow only when a small voltage is applied to the base. The arrows in the diagram show conventional current flow, which occurs in the opposite direction to electron flow.*

NPN BIPOLAR JUNCTION TRANSISTOR

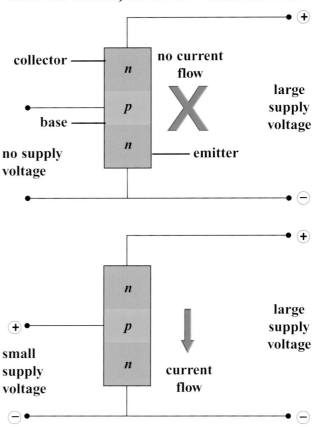

holes tend to flow to the negative terminal. In other words, the current carriers flow away from the *pn* junction in opposite directions. Thus no current can flow in the circuit.

When the terminals are reversed, the electrons from the *n* region again tend to flow to the positive terminal, but to do so, they must pass across the junction in the opposite direction. Current now flows through the circuit.

Thus the *pn* junction allows electrical current to pass only in one direction. A device with such a junction is known as a diode. It is the simplest semiconductor device and is a vital component of modern electronic circuits.

Transistors

In 1947, U.S. physicists John Bardeen (1908–1991), Walter Brattain (1902–1987), and William Shockley (1910–1989) developed the transistor. In one type, called the bipolar junction transistor (BJT), three layers of *n*-type and *p*-type semiconductor materials are sandwiched together,

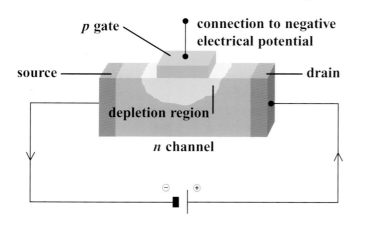

either as an *npn* structure (see the illustration above) or as a *pnp* structure. In an *npn* transistor, the thin *p* region is called the base, one *n* region is the emitter, and the other *n* region is the collector. When a separate, variable, positive voltage is applied to the *p*-layer base, electrons flow from the negatively charged emitter to the *p*-layer base. If the *p* region is sufficiently thin, the electrons will pass right through to the positively charged collector. The strength of the current produced at the collector depends on the positive charge at the base.

◀ *In a junction field effect transistor (JFET), electrons can usually flow from the source to the drain through a block, or channel, of n-type semiconductor. However, some electrons from the n channel also diffuse into a layer of p-type semiconductor (the p gate) above it, creating a depletion region in which there are no charge carriers. The depletion region can be expanded if the p gate is held at a negative electrical potential. This removes further electrons from the n channel, allowing the transistor to finely control tiny currents to sensitive integrated circuits.*

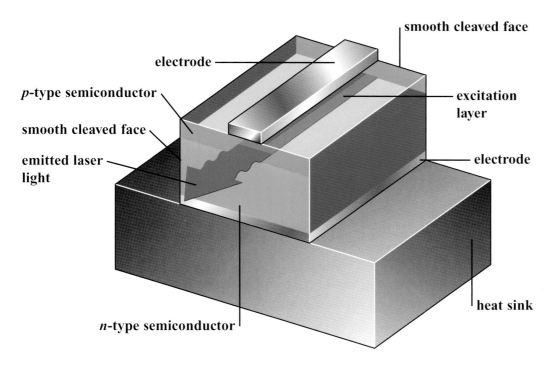

electrode

p-type semiconductor

smooth cleaved face

emitted laser light

n-type semiconductor

smooth cleaved face

excitation layer

electrode

heat sink

◀ *A semiconductor laser produces photons of light from the junction between an n-type and a p-type semiconductor.*

In another type of transistor, called the field effect transistor (FET), a channel of either *n*-type or *p*-type material is placed between two heavily doped areas of the same material. These areas are called the source and the drain (comparable to the emitter and collector of a BJT). The FET uses voltage to control an electrostatic field within the transistor. By increasing the voltage applied to the gate above the channel, the size of the depletion region near the gate can be increased, thus reducing the ability of the channel to conduct current.

One type of FET, called the junction FET (JFET), operates only as a depletion device (see the illustration at the bottom of page 1542). Voltages applied to the gate deplete charge carriers in the channel so that conduction can no longer occur between the source and the drain.

Depending on the way in which transistors are wired into circuits, they can act as amplifiers, oscillators, or switches. Their great advantage is that they are small, very tough, need little current, and give out little heat.

Thyristors, LEDs, and lasers

Thyristors are formed by sandwiching four layers of semiconductor material together in a *pnpn* arrangement. They are now widely used in control and switching devices, such as television remote controls, motor-driven equipment, and heating and lighting circuits. Light-sensitive semiconductors are also important parts of photoelectric cells. A similar use is in solar cells, which consist of semiconductors that convert solar radiation into electricity.

One type of semiconductor also does the reverse—it generates light when a current passes through it. It is called a light-emitting diode (LED) and is widely used in digital devices. Gallium arsenide is a semiconductor often used as an LED. Lasers made from gallium arsenide are also finding widespread use in fiber-optic communications.

The silicon chip

In the 1960s, scientists found that they could make transistors from a single slice of silicon, and the silicon chip was born. In the chip, each *n* region or *p* region is formed on the same slice by doping different areas with different dopants. In this way, entire circuits can be made on one chip. It is now possible to cram thousands of components into a wafer-thin chip a few millimeters square.

See also: ATOM AND MOLECULE • MICROELECTRONICS • SILICON • TRANSISTOR

Servomechanism

A servomechanism is an automatic control device that has many uses in industry and transportation. These devices are used to control machine tools and many production processes. Servomechanisms also help steer ships, fly airplanes and spacecraft, and navigate submarines underwater.

There are many different kinds of control systems. A rudder is used to control a ship, for example, and a steering wheel is used to control an automobile. A large vehicle is hard to steer with hand power alone, and so power assistance is usually provided. A unit in the steering mechanism uses power from the engine to build up the force put on the steering wheel. The extra power passes to the steering mechanism to turn the wheels.

In this example, a small muscular force is being used to control the powerful engine force. This is called servoassistance, and it is one feature of devices called servomechanisms. However, servo-steering is not a servomechanism in itself. To stay on course, the driver steers the vehicle all the time. When the vehicle veers off course, the driver turns the wheel to bring it back on course.

Imagine a device that could turn the wheel automatically every time the vehicle veered off course. This is a true servomechanism. Automatic control is the other vital feature of a servomechanism.

Fantails
One of the earliest self-controlling mechanisms was the windmill fantail. To keep going at full power, a windmill needed to be kept with its sails facing into the wind. With early windmills, the miller had to move the body of the mill around each time the wind changed direction.

In the mid-eighteenth century, the fantail was invented. This device was a small fan that turned at right angles to the main sails. It was attached to a cap on top of the windmill, which also carried the main sails. With the sails into the wind, the fantail was still. When the wind direction changed, the fantail also turned. Through a series of gears, the fantail turned the mill cap until the sails faced into the wind again. The process was fully automatic.

The governor
In 1788, Scottish engineer James Watt (1736–1819) invented an even more important self-regulating device called the steam-engine governor. The steam-engine governor consists of an upright rod that is driven around by the steam engine. Heavy balls hang from smaller movable rods linked to the main rod. At the bottom they are attached by more linkages to a collar that can slide up and down the main rod. Another link connects the collar to the valve, and this allows steam to enter the engine.

▶ *One of the best-known uses for servomechanisms is in the autopilot systems of airplanes. Airliners fly on autopilot for much of the journey, so the human pilot does not have to keep the plane on a steady course throughout the duration of the flight.*

When the engine runs, the main rod spins around, and the balls move outward by centrifugal force (they tend to fly out from the center). They also move upward, pulling the collar with them. The collar lifts the rod that works the steam valve. The mechanism is adjusted so that the engine runs at the speed the driver wants. If the engine speeds up, the balls move farther out and up. The collar then lifts the valve linkage and closes the valve slightly. This reduces the amount of steam going into the engine, and the engine speed falls. If the engine speed falls too much, however, the balls drop. This opens the steam valve wider, more steam enters the engine, and the engine speeds up.

After each speed change, the engine may overshoot the desired position of equilibrium (balance). The mechanism would then have to go into reverse to correct the imbalance. It would start wobbling around the equilibrium position. This process is called "hunting." It is not a good idea to make a servomechanism overly sensitive; otherwise a lot of hunting may occur.

Feedback control

Like all servomechanisms, the governor works by what is known as feedback control. For control, it relies on receiving information about how the device it is regulating is actually behaving and compares this with how it should behave (the right speed setting). If there is a difference, a signal is sent to adjust the steam valve to correct the error.

Automatic pilots

The autopilot systems of airplanes have servomechanisms connected to three control surfaces. The ailerons control rolling, the elevators control pitching, and the rudder controls yawing and heading. Each servomechanism has similar parts. It has a sensor that can tell if the plane is straying away from the right path or height. It compares what it senses with a gyroscope, which always points in the same direction. When an error is found, a signal is sent to a servomotor, which moves one or more of the control devices until the airplane is flying in the right way again.

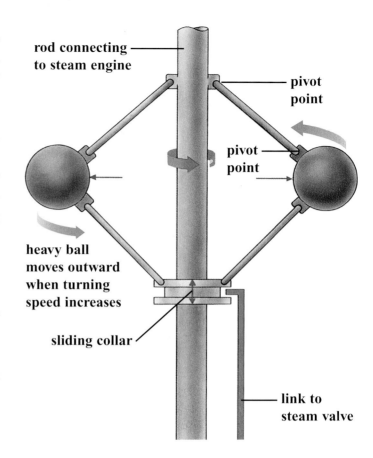

rod connecting to steam engine

pivot point

pivot point

heavy ball moves outward when turning speed increases

sliding collar

link to steam valve

▲ *The steam-engine governor is an early example of a servomechanism. As the speed of the steam engine rises or falls, the up or down movement of the balls closes or opens the steam valve.*

Ships also use autopilots, which are simpler than those found in airplanes, because ships move only on the surface of the sea. The main sensing element is the gyrocompass, which sends out error signals that control a servomotor linked to the rudder.

A more advanced system is needed by submarines and spacecraft because there are no landmarks that can be used to help them steer in the right direction. These craft have an inertial navigation system. This system includes three gyroscopes and three accelerometers to sense changes in speed in three dimensions. A computer analyzes the signals and calculates any correction that may be needed to keep the craft on course.

See also: AIRPLANE • GEAR • GYROSCOPE • SHIP AND SHIPBUILDING • SUBMARINE • WINDMILL AND WIND PUMP

Sewage treatment

Sewage is liquid and solid waste carried off in sewers and drains. Sewage that is taken away from houses or factories eventually finds its way to the rivers, and from there to the sea. However, the sewage must first be treated to clean it. Some of the byproducts are useful as fertilizer, fuel, or for breaking down other sewage.

The need to clean up sewage was first recognized around the time of the Industrial Revolution (1760–1840). At first, soil was used to treat sewage. Human and animal waste contains nitrogen, which can be broken down by tiny microorganisms in soil and used as fertilizer. By pouring sewage onto the land, the water could, to some extent, be purified.

However, too much fertilizer may be bad for the soil, unless the right crops are grown as part of the farming cycle. As populations grew, and with them the amount of sewage, the "sewage farms," as they were known, became less able to do the job. Generally, at least 100 acres (40 hectares) of land would be needed to adequately treat 1 million gallons (4.5 million liters) of sewage. This amount of sewage is produced every day by a population of about 20,000.

In 1898, a Royal Commission was set up in Britain to study how best to dispose of sewage. The commission decided that the disposal of sewage into rivers and streams should be much more strictly controlled and recommended that new ways of purifying sewage be found that did not mean using more and more land.

Precipitation

One new method of treating sewage was chemical precipitation. This involved treating the sewage with a small amount of an iron or aluminum compound, and then adding lime (calcium

▼ *This sewage-treatment plant outside Cape Town, South Africa, is typical of many around the world. These plants treat the sewage produced by people and industry to make it less harmful to dispose.*

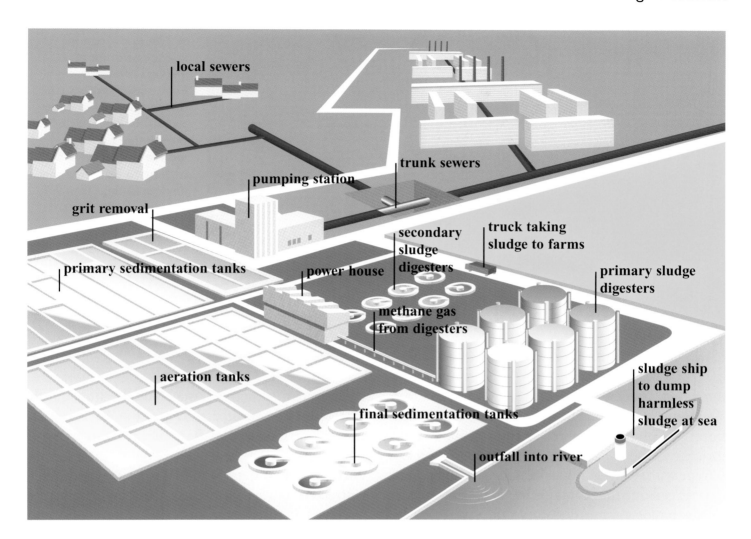

▲ This is a diagram of a modern sewage plant. Waste from homes and industry are treated at sites like these. The sludge produced by sewage plants can be used as fertilizer, incinerated to generate power, or simply dumped in the ocean.

carbonate; $CaCO_3$). When the sewage was passed through large tanks, the metal hydroxide that formed would sink to the bottom, taking a lot of the impurities (waste) in the sewage with it. The remaining effluent (liquid sewage) could then be treated more easily on land. In turn, this built up great amounts of foul-smelling sludge in the tanks that had to be removed every couple of days.

A different idea lay behind the biological filter, which is used for the second-stage treatment of sewage. A basin with walls 5 to 6 feet (1.5 to 1.8 meters) deep is filled with hard coke (a form of carbon) or other permeable material. A sloping floor allows the liquid to drain away easily.

When the treated sewage is sprayed onto this filter bed, it is broken down by microorganisms such as bacteria. This results in the impurities being oxidized. Thus carbon, which is found in all living matter and plant and animal waste, is oxidized to carbon dioxide (CO_2). Nitrogen combines with oxygen to form nitrate compounds.

DID YOU KNOW?

Effective sewage treatment is vital in the control of disease. Many potentially fatal diseases are carried in water, and they thrive in stagnant bodies of raw sewage. In many regions of the developing world, poor sanitation results in a high number of cases of waterborne diseases such as cholera, dysentery, hepatitis, and typhoid.

◄ *The first stage in sewage treatment involves removing any large solid masses such as trash, using large bar screens at the ends of the sewage pipes. At a later stage, workers skim settling tanks to remove any remaining particles.*

Activated sludge process

This stage of the purification process was further improved by the discovery of the activated sludge process in 1916. This process involves mixing sewage with what is known as activated sludge. This is a sticky slime that contains the organisms needed for the biological purification of the sewage.

The mixture is passed through tanks through which air is always traveling. The sewage and the organisms are kept together for about ten hours so the impurities in the sewage can be biologically oxidized. The activated sludge settles out in tanks, and the purified sewage is discharged into a river.

Purifying the water

Untreated sewage contains not only impurities dissolved in the water, but also much solid and semisolid matter. This is because it comes from a variety of places: washbasins, toilets, bathrooms, and kitchens, as well as a great many industrial

▶ *In this municipal sewage treatment plant in Austin, Texas, equipment is employed to churn and aerate compost produced by mixing sewage and sludge and organic materials such as tree trimmings and lawn wastes. After the recycled material is aged for a few weeks, it is packed and sold as fertilizer in garden stores.*

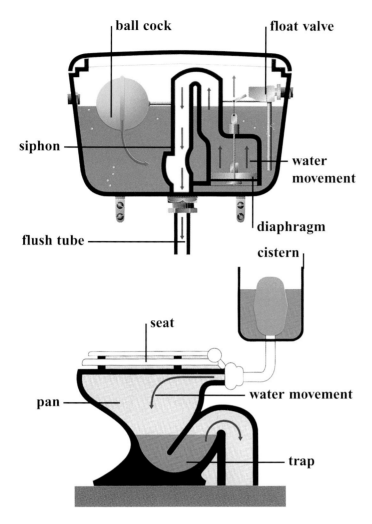

ball cock

float valve

siphon

water movement

flush tube

diaphragm

cistern

seat

water movement

pan

trap

◀ *The flush lever on a toilet raises a diaphragm in the cistern, which causes water to be pushed into the pan by atmospheric pressure. The contents of the pan are pushed through the trap by the incoming water.*

In the next step, the finer dirt in sewage settles to the bottom of sedimentation tanks. This sludge is pumped to a machine that removes water and thus thickened. Then it is treated with chemicals and pressed to form "cakes" for use as fertilizer.

Digestion of the sludge

Thickened sludge may also be heated in an anaerobic (oxygen-free) digestion chamber, where it is broken down biologically and made suitable for spraying onto land as fertilizer. This process also produces methane gas (CH_4), which is collected for use as a fuel.

The sewage left after the sludge has been removed is then treated using biological filters or the activated sludge process. The resulting liquid sewage then passes through the final settling tanks to remove any sediment (silt) that may have formed. This sediment, which contains the micro-organisms that break down the sewage, is returned to the system to keep the biological processes going. The treated sewage may be strained further before being discharged into the river.

Other systems

One of the simplest forms of sewage disposal is the cesspool, which is used mainly in remote country areas. This consists of a tank or pit into which sewage is drained. It has to be emptied two or three times a month and must be kept watertight so as not to leak into the main water supply.

A better choice is the septic tank. This breaks down the sewage biologically, using some of the sludge produced to keep the activity going.

In coastal areas, sewage is sometimes poured directly into the sea or, more often, treated first and watered down to avoid too much pollution.

processes. However, the water simply carries all the polluting matter; it is not itself changed. Thus, it ought to be possible to remove all the pollutants and restore the water to its original pure state. In practice, over 90 percent purification is often achieved, but this figure depends on the source of the sewage. Complex artificial chemicals found in industrial waste are very difficult to remove from sewage, and there are concerns regarding the ability of sewage-treatment plants to be able to do this.

Modern treatment

In modern treatment plants, sewage first goes through bar screens to remove large solid masses. The solid masses are either burned in an incinerator or broken up and put back into the sewage. Then grit, which could damage the pumps or other equipment, is separated out of the sewage mechanically and dumped.

See also: FERTILIZER • OXIDATION AND REDUCTION • POLLUTION

Ship and shipbuilding

People have traveled from place to place along rivers and across oceans for thousands of years. The vessels used to travel on water changed considerably at the end of the nineteenth century, first with the invention of the steam engine and then with gasoline- and diesel-powered engines. In the twenty-first century, new shipbuilding materials offer alternatives to iron and steel.

A ship is any large floating vessel that is capable of deep-water navigation and crossing open water (seas and oceans). A boat is generally a smaller craft, or a vessel of any size restricted to inland waterways. Historically, the term *ship* was applied to a sailing vessel that had three or more masts. Nowadays, the term refers to a vessel of more than 500 tons (454 tonnes).

How ships float

When a ship slides into the water, it sinks a little way and then floats. The weight of the ship pushes aside (displaces) some water. The weight of this water is equal to the weight of the ship. However, a ship can only displace as much water as its own volume. If a ship is loaded with too much weight, the volume of water that the ship is able to displace will not weigh as much as the ship, and the ship will sink. All ships have a maximum laden (loaded) weight limit, above which the vessel will sink dangerously low in the water.

Stability

A ship must stay upright in the water. If it is likely to capsize (turn upside down), it is unstable. The action between the weight of the ship pushing

▼ *Cruise ships are some of the most impressive examples of shipbuilding. These massive ships are designed to carry thousands of people, often in great luxury.*

► *If large cargo ships such as supertankers sink, they can cause widespread environmental disaster. It is important, therefore, that their designs and construction make them as stable and structurally sound as possible.*

downward and its buoyancy (ability to float in the water) pushing upward is what produces a stable or unstable ship. The weight of a ship is spread throughout the structure, but it acts as though it were all pushing straight downward in one spot. This spot is called the center of gravity.

The location of the center of gravity depends on the way in which the weight is spread around the ship. If most of the weight is toward the bottom of the ship, the center of gravity will be low down. If the weight is mostly high up, the center of gravity will be high, too. However high or low it may be, the center of gravity is always on the center line of the ship, midway between the sides.

The buoyancy forces of the water push on the underwater part of the hull from all sides. This buoyancy also acts as though it were all pushing straight upward on a single spot in the ship. This spot is called the center of buoyancy. This is on the center line of the ship as long as the ship is upright but moves over to one side when the ship heels (leans) over. When the ship is upright, the forces of gravity and buoyancy cancel each other out.

As the ship heels over, the forces of gravity and buoyancy still act straight up and down. However, now they are not on the same vertical line, so they no longer cancel each other out.

The point where the buoyancy force, acting straight upward, meets the center line of the ship is called the metacenter. If the metacenter is above the center of gravity, the forces will act together to bring the ship upright once again. The ship is stable in this case. However, if the metacenter is below the center of gravity, the two forces act together to push the ship farther over, until it may capsize altogether.

The positions of the centers of gravity and buoyancy and of the metacenter are carefully calculated by naval architects to ensure vessels will be stable at sea. Keeping the center of gravity as low as possible is a good idea. This is why ships carry ballast—extra weight loaded low down in the ship—particularly when there is no cargo. Many ships now have their upper parts made of light aluminum alloys for the same reason.

EARLY BOATS AND SHIPS

The first water craft were rafts made from wood or reeds and dugouts made from hollowed-out logs. Dugouts were first used in Europe and Asia around eight thousand years ago. A problem with dugouts is that they can capsize easily, so their stability was increased by adding outriggers—floats attached to the dugout by arms. Dugouts were further improved by adding planks, called washboards, up

► *This cutaway of a carvel-built wooden boat shows its traditional construction. The boat is built from the keel up, and the forepost is extended from one end to form the bow. Ribs, gunwales, and thwarts (cross braces) are then built around these two main elements. Finally, a deck is added, and the cladding planks, often shaped by heating and bending with steam, are nailed on edge to edge.*

TRADITIONAL CARVEL CONSTRUCTION

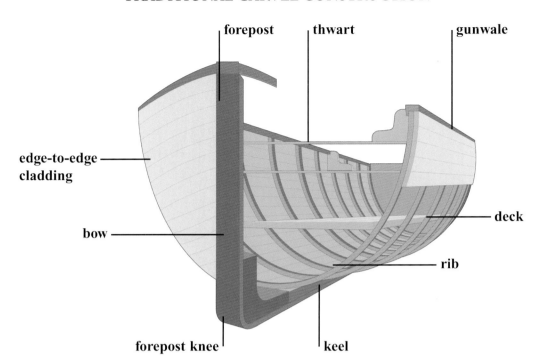

forepost · thwart · gunwale

edge-to-edge cladding

bow

deck

rib

forepost knee · keel

their sides to provide them with more height in the water. These simple wooden vessels were some of the first boats.

The ancient Egyptians lashed bundles of reeds together to form rafts. Then they began to pull the ends up with ropes to shape the rafts into boats.

The Mesopotamians, who lived in present-day Iraq around the time of the ancient Egyptians, used wood, animal skins, and bark to make boats. They covered a wooden hull with skins and bark and made it watertight with resin or a tarlike substance called bitumen. Similar boats were built in Scandinavia about two thousand years later, and the Viking longboats of the fourth century were also made in this way. The Native American canoe and kayak are similar to these early wood-and-skin boats.

The Chinese also started with rafts, probably about 4000 BCE, but they were made of bamboo. At a later date, perhaps about 1000 BCE, the Chinese began to adapt the raft by laying the bamboo along the curved sides of a series of semicircular wooden planks. Finally, by replacing the bamboo with planks, the Chinese made the first plank-constructed boats. This method of construction was soon adopted worldwide.

Plank construction

Building boats and ships from lengths (planks) of wood is a highly skilled craft in which numerous wooden pieces are used to build a strong, stable, and watertight hull. This method of construction developed in Europe during the Middle Ages and was the way in which most boats and ships were built up until the early nineteenth century, when the dawn of the Industrial Revolution in Britain saw the first iron ships being constructed. The two styles of plank construction are clinker and carvel.

In a clinker-built vessel, the shape of the hull is formed by bending and fixing planks around one or more mold pieces. The main feature of this type of construction is that the planks overlap. After the planking has been completed, light wooden frames are fixed to the interior of the hull to strap the planking together. Clinker construction is normally used only for small, light craft, such as rowboats.

Carvel construction is used for building large boats and ships. In carvel construction, wooden planks are fitted edge to edge over a completed framework. This determines the shape of the hull and also supports the structure. The framework consists of a piece called the keel, ribs, and decks.

DID YOU KNOW?

Some U.S. Navy aircraft carriers use nuclear power. This gives them an enormous range without needing to refuel, so they can stay at sea for extended periods. A nuclear ship uses heat from a nuclear reactor to make steam, which drives steam turbines.

The keel runs along the bottom of the ship and holds the ribs and decks together. The frames are strapped together inside with full-length planks called stringers. To make the ship watertight, a sealing material called calking compound is put between the outside planks.

RECENT SHIPBUILDING

The first shipbuilders found it impossible to make ships as large as modern ships. The strength of their carvel-built ships was in their keel—the beam that effectively held the ribs, decks, and the rest of the ship together. The keel was always made out of one single tree, so the only way to build a larger ship was to find a taller tree. Early shipbuilders could not find a strong enough way of joining two trees together at their ends to make a longer keel. Whenever they tried, the ships broke in half in heavy seas.

Eventually, ships were built in which all the parts helped support each other, just as a strong basket can be made out of easily bent canes. These web-frame ships did not need to rely on the keel for the strength of the entire ship. However, wooden ships could still not be built much longer than about 260 feet (80 meters). It was not until shipbuilders began using iron and steel that longer ships could be built. Even with these ships, however, there is still a risk of breaking in half, particularly with the huge supertankers. The longer the ship, the greater the likelihood of it breaking up in a storm. To avoid this, large ships, such as supertankers, are often made very wide instead of long. However, this brings other problems. A wide ship will need more engine power to push it through the water, and ships that are too wide will not be able to use narrow waterways such as the Panama Canal.

Iron began to take over from wood for shipbuilding during the Industrial Revolution. Because of iron's strength, iron ships could be much larger than wooden ships. Also, iron frames took up less room than wooden frames, so iron ships had more space for carrying cargo. Another benefit was that iron ships did not need as much maintenance as wooden ships.

In the 1880s, steel began to be used instead of iron for shipbuilding. Steel is stronger and more durable than iron, so steel ships could be made lighter than iron ships but just as strong. Most modern ships are made from steel.

By the end of the twentieth century, metal alloys (mixtures of metals), plastics, and composites (combination materials) had been developed for shipbuilding, although these materials are not all suitable for very large ships. Many high-performance ships are built from lightweight, aluminum alloy, and specialist ships, such as navy minesweepers, are made from glass-reinforced plastic (GRP). This material is both light and nonmagnetic, so it protects the ship from magnetic mines.

▼ *This cutaway watercolour drawing shows PSS* **Great Eastern,** *built in London, England, between 1853 and 1858.* **Great Eastern** *was built of iron, measured 692 feet (211 meters) long, and had accommodation for four thousand passengers.*

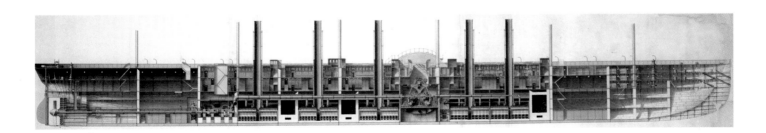

◀ *The USS* Mason, *a navy destroyer, undergoes outfitting in a floating dry dock in Bath, Maine, prior to entering service. The floating dry dock will submerge to release the ship.*

Fabrication

Originally, metal ships were made by rivetting all the different parts together. Every ship was constructed on a building berth. First, the keel was laid, then the frames or ribs were erected, the floors were put in place, and the structure was held together by long pieces of wood called ribbands. Metal plating was then added over the frame, and all the parts of the structure were rivetted together. This method was very similar to the keel-up construction of wooden ships.

In modern ship construction, large sections of the ship are first constructed separately. Each of these sections—for example, the bow or stern—is built up from subassemblies or component parts, which are then welded together to make the complete section. The sections are manufactured under cover in large sheds some distance from the building berth. As each section is completed, it is transported to the berth and welded to the adjacent section. This method of construction has many advantages. Much work can continue undercover during bad weather, and subassemblies and component parts can be built in sequences to suit the welding operations.

Propulsion

As well as bringing the first metal-hulled ships, the Industrial Revolution also brought the combustion engine. First the steam engine, and then steam turbine, gasoline, diesel, and gas turbine engines revolutionized maritime transportation.

Before the Industrial Revolution, all ships had sails. With combustion engines came first paddle wheels, and then from the 1840s, screw propellers. Propellers are still used on most ships.

Steam turbines began to take over from steam engines in the late nineteenth century. By the early twentieth century, diesel engines were being used in ships. Most modern ships are powered by steam turbines or diesel engines. Gasoline engines tend to be found only in smaller boats because of the lower cost and superior energy efficiency of diesel.

Some modern high-speed ships are driven by gas turbines. Gas-turbine engines are less fuel efficient than diesel engines, and they are used only when low weight and high power output is necessary.

A recent form of propulsion that is becoming popular on many types of ships is electric propulsion. Large electric motors are connected directly to propellers and powered by a generator inside the ship. These electric propulsor units are more efficient and less expensive to maintain than combustion engines.

TYPES OF SHIPS

Modern merchant ships are generally one of four types: oil tankers, dry cargo vessels, bulk carriers, and container ships.

Oil tankers

Oil tankers have taken over from the great passenger liners of the past as the giants of the oceans. They are made as large as possible because many of the costs of running a ship are the same whatever the size. For example, tankers only require a small crew, and their cost will be the same no matter how large the ship.

All tankers have the engines, bridge, and crew quarters at the stern (back). This part of the ship will have a double bottom for safety. An empty space lies between this part of the ship and the oil cargo to prevent oil from leaking directly into the crew quarters. The rest of the ship contains several tanks for the oil. The tanks are separated so that if one is punctured, the ship will not sink, and the cargo will not be lost. Also, a different kind of oil can be carried in each tank.

Dry cargo vessels

Most ships carrying general cargo are built with the engines and crew quarters in the middle of the ship or toward the stern. The majority of each ship is taken up by a number of holds, large spaces where the cargo is stowed. The cargo is lowered by crane through hatches in the deck.

Dry cargo ships carry some cranes of their own on deck in case a dock has no suitable ones for loading or unloading. Some dry cargo ships will have some small tanks for bulk cargo such as grain or vegetable oil.

Bulk carriers

Ships built to carry cargo that can be poured into tanks are called bulk carriers. Such cargo may be sugar or wheat, or metal ores for refining. Bulk

▲ The largest ships are cargo ships, which transport goods throughout the world. Loose goods, such as grain and oil, are stored in tanks or holds, while other goods are transported in containers.

carriers are arranged in a similar way to oil tankers but almost always have a double bottom over the entire ship. They also have wing tanks to carry water as ballast when the ship is running empty.

Container ships

Containers are large steel boxes, similar to a big truck without the cab and the wheels. They are packed with goods in a factory, taken by road to the docks, and loaded onto a specially designed ship.

The advantage of a container is that the goods are packed at the factory and not disturbed until they arrive at their destination. The containers, always the same size, are lifted on and off trucks, trains, and ships by cranes designed for the job. Thus, handling costs are much less than for goods packed in boxes or bundles of different shapes and sizes.

Container ships have holds of just the right size to take the standard containers. All the cranes and handling machinery are adapted to deal with the containers quickly and easily. Most containers are stowed in holds, but some are carried on deck.

See also: MARINE PROPULSION •
NAVIGATION • TANKER • WARSHIP

Silicon

Silicon is the second most common element found on Earth, after oxygen. It is present in most rocks and in sand and clay. Silicon is a semiconductor, which makes it useful for transistors and other electronic equipment. Silicon is an important ingredient for glass and pottery and is used in rubber, sealants, and insulation.

In its pure form, silicon is a dull gray solid that shines in a similar way to most metals. However, silicon is not a metal but a metalloid. Metalloids share characteristics with both metals, such as iron, and nonmetals, such as sulfur.

Semiconductors

The most useful characteristics of metalloids, especially silicon, is that they are semiconductors. In pure form, semiconductors are poor conductors of electricity, but their conductivity changes when certain impurities are added. By placing different types of impurities in different regions of the semiconductor, scientists can make important devices such as switches and rectifiers, which allow current to flow in one direction only.

Semiconductor devices can be small, and a single chip may contain a circuit with many thousands of transistors. Such chips are the basis for modern communications and computer technology.

Natural compounds

Pure silicon is not found in nature. It is always found as compounds (combinations of different elements). The most common silicon compound is silica (silicon dioxide; SiO_2). Sand grains and quartz are natural forms of silica. The gemstones opal and jasper are made mainly from silica. Their bright colors are produced by different impurities.

Silicon combined with oxygen and a metal is called a silicate. Silicates are found in rocks such as the mineral mica and the gemstone garnet.

Most pure silicon is made by heating silica in a furnace using a carbon-rich fuel, such as coal. The oxygen and carbon combine to form carbon dioxide (CO_2), which escapes into the air. Almost completely pure silicon is left behind.

Uses of silica

Silica is not just used to make pure silicon. Its main use is in the glass-making industry and for making pottery. After silica has been melted, it cools to form a colorless glass that can be molded and pulled into any shape before it hardens completely.

◀ *This disk of pure silicon has hundreds of separate integrated circuits, or chips, etched onto its surface. These chips are made in a clean environment to stop specks of dust from causing flaws in the circuits.*

▲ *Silica, or silicon dioxide, is used to make the tiles that cover parts of the space shuttle. These tiles are resistant to heat and protect the shuttle as it flies into Earth's atmosphere from space. The air rubbing past the spacecraft produces a lot of heat, and the shuttle would burn up if it were not covered with tiles.*

These quartz crystals are piezoelectric—they vibrate (wobble rhythmically) when electrified. A quartz clock measures time passing by counting the the regular vibrations of a quartz crystal.

Silica is also made into aerogels. These cloudy solids are very light mixtures of silica and air. They look like wisps of smoke. Aerogels are highly resistant to heat and are used as insulators.

Silicones

Silicones are artificial polymers, consisting mainly of silicon, carbon, and oxygen. Polymers are compounds that are made up of long chains of smaller molecules, called monomers. Silicones can be hard or flexible solids, or thick liquids.

Silicone rubber is strong and stretchy and can be pressed into any shape. It is often used to insulate electrical items. Liquid silicones are waterproof, and they are used to seal cracks in windows and bathrooms. The liquid dries to form a flexible solid.

DID YOU KNOW?

Most of the world's silicon chips are made in Silicon Valley in California. This area stretches south of San Francisco from Palo Alto to San Jose. Many of the world's largest computer companies are based there, including Apple, Hewlett Packard, and Intel. Silicon chips have been made in Silicon Valley since the 1960s. At first, they were used mainly in digital watches and calculators. Now silicon chips are smaller and more powerful and are used in computers, cell phones, and music players.

Silicones are also used to make artificial body parts, such as replacement heart valves and breast implants. These items are fitted by a surgeon. The advantage of using silicone items in this way is that the human body does not reject the silicone object as it does other foreign materials.

See also: GLASS • PIEZOELECTRICITY • POLYMERIZATION • SEMICONDUCTOR

Silver

Silver is a brilliant, shining white precious metal. It has been prized by people for thousands of years and has been found in tombs dating back to 4000 BCE. The greatest use of silver today is in photography, where it is used to coat and develop photographic film. It is also used for coins, jewelry, ornaments, and eating utensils.

Silver is a rare metal, and very little exists in Earth's crust. Pure deposits of silver do exist, but most of the metal is found mixed with other elements in the form of compounds called minerals. The most important silver mineral is called argentine (silver sulfide; Ag_2S). Silver is also found in combination with gold as a naturally occurring alloy (mixture of metals) called electrum. Silver minerals are found in most parts of the world. The largest deposits exist in the Americas—Colorado, Idaho, and Nevada in the United States, and also in Bolivia, Canada, Mexico, and Peru. Australia, China, and Poland are also important silver producers.

Special characteristics

Silver has many unusual properties. The pure metal conducts both heat and electricity better than any other material. It is also very resistant to corrosion. The reflective properties of silver are exploited in the manufacture of mirrors and other applications in which protection from the Sun's rays is needed. For example, silver was used to protect the *Magellan* spacecraft from overheating as it orbited the planet Venus. Venus is much closer to the Sun than Earth, and the *Magellan* spacecraft faced high levels of solar radiation during the orbit.

▶ *A foundry worker casts ingots of pure silver at the American Smelting and Refining Plant in Selby, California. Pure silver is highly prized for its beauty and value, but it is also often mixed with other metals to improve its hardness or other physical characteristics.*

▲ *Sixteenth-century silversmiths cast and shape pure silver into coins. From the end of the Roman Empire until the sixteenth century, almost all coins were made of silver due to a severe shortage of gold.*

Mining and refining

Silver minerals are usually mixed with the minerals of other metals such as copper, lead, tin, and zinc. It is by mining and refining (purifying) these minerals that most silver is now obtained.

Soon after Spanish explorers opened up the Mexican silver mines in the 1520s, they developed the patio process to refine silver minerals from the rocks in which they were found. The mineral-rich rocks were first crushed into a fine powder and mixed with common salt (sodium chloride; $NaCl$). The rock and salt mixture was then roasted with copper sulfide (CuS) and water. The resulting mudlike paste was spread over a patio (paved yard). Mercury was then added, and heat from the Sun helped the mercury reduce the silver from the paste. Unfortunately, the patio process wasted large amounts of mercury. Gradually, better ways were found of refining silver.

Modern methods

The von Patera method of refining silver involves heating the silver minerals with 7 percent rock salt to form silver chloride. The silver is then extracted by adding sodium hydrosulfite ($Na_2S_2O_4$) solution.

Another method, called the cyanide process, involves crushing and mixing the silver minerals with sodium cyanide ($NaCN$) solution. The silver dissolves in the solution, and zinc dust is added to the liquid, which causes the silver to settle. The silver is then filtered out, melted, and cast into ingots.

Silver as a by-product

Many metals, such as copper, nickel, and zinc, contain silver as an impurity. These metals are purified by electrolysis. Since the silver (and other precious metals such as gold and platinum group metals) does not dissolve in the electrolyte fluid, it sinks in the tank as part of the slime of impurities. The slime is then treated to remove as much of the copper, nickel, and zinc as possible. The slime is then made into anode blocks, which are then put into a solution of silver nitrate ($AgNO_3$). During electrolysis, the silver in the anode blocks migrates to the cathodes, which are made from carbon or pure silver. All the nonsilver metals in the anodes settle as slime so that they, too, can be collected and the metals removed. The silver produced by electrolysis is almost 100 percent pure.

DID YOU KNOW?

One of the more unusual uses for silver and its compounds is as an antibacterial agent to prevent infection. Historical records show that the ancient Greeks and Romans used silver as a disinfectant for water. More recently, in 1884, German physician F. Crede used silver nitrate as an eyedrop for newborn babies, reducing the number of cases of infant blindness. The treatment was so successful that it continued right up until the development of antibiotics in the 1940s. A silver compound called sulfadiazine is now used to speed up the regrowth of damaged skin in cases of major burns. Some physicians also believe that silver may be useful in the treatment of certain types of cancers.

◀ *Artisans shape pieces of silver into items of jewelry. Silver is a fairly malleable metal, which means that it is easy to work into different shapes and to mark with intricate designs.*

Silver purity

Pure silver is not completely pure—it is too soft for most of its uses. Instead, the silver is mixed with 7.5 percent copper to form an alloy called sterling silver. Silver is expensive, so the amount of silver in alloys such as sterling silver is regulated. In Britain, there are four levels of purity, called fineness levels. Pure silver has a fineness of 999—it contains 999 parts per thousand (99.9 percent pure). The lowest level is 800 fineness (80 percent pure). Sterling silver has a fineness of 925.

Silver plate

Silver is often used to coat cheaper metals. In a process called electroplating, a thin layer of silver plate is added to the surface of the cheaper metal using electricity. An alloy of copper, nickel, and zinc is the best metal for silver plating. The thin layer of silver plate is marked as EPNS, which means "electroplated nickel silver."

DID YOU KNOW?

Many thousands of tons of silver are produced each year from recycling. The most important source of recycled silver is from the photographic industry.

Before electroplating came into use in 1840, silver plate items were made by sandwiching copper between two layers of silver and fixing them together by fusion (melting). The method, called Sheffield plate, was developed by an Englishman named Thomas Bolsover.

Staining and cleaning

Silver does not rust or tarnish in clean air. Sulfur, contained in the fumes of coal and gas fires, does cause silver items to turn brown. Foods containing sulfur, such as cabbages, also tarnish silver tableware. A thin film of silver sulfide forms on the surface of the silver as it reacts with the sulfur.

Photography

Large amounts of silver are used by the photographic industry. When silver is combined with elements called halogens, salts are formed that react to light. When light strikes silver chloride ($AgCl$) and silver bromide ($AgBr$), for example, the compounds are converted into metallic silver. When these compounds are impregnated on film and exposed to light, they can be used to record visual images in the form of photographs.

See also: ELECTROLYSIS • METAL • PHOTOGRAPHY

Skeletal system

Skeletons are what give animal bodies their shape. They also provide a solid platform for muscles to push against. Humans and other large animals have internal skeletons made of bone. Most smaller animals, such as insects, snails, and crabs, however, have skeletons that are on the outside of their bodies. Most skeletons are made of solid substances. However, worms and jellyfish have skeletons made of water.

The main role of a skeleton is to provide a solid object for an animal's muscles to push against and make the body move. Without the skeleton, the muscles would just pull a body out of shape into a useless mass of muscle and fat.

Skeleton types

Most skeletons are made from hard, solid materials. Humans and other vertebrates (organisms with backbones), such as whales, birds, and snakes, have skeletons made of bones. The bones are located inside the body and surrounded by muscles. When a muscle contracts (shortens), it pulls against the solid bone and causes a part of the body to move. Some vertebrates, such as sharks and other similar fish, do not have bony skeletons. Instead, their skeletons are made of cartilage. This is a bendy substance that is also found in the bodies of other vertebrates alongside bone. For example, a person's nose and ears consist mainly of cartilage.

Other animals, such as insects and snails, do not have skeletons inside their bodies. Instead, they have skeletons on the outside, which are called exoskeletons. An example of an exoskeleton is a crab's shell. The animal's muscles are inside the shell and pull against it in the same way as the muscles in a person's body pull on bones. Most exoskeletons are made from a flexible substance called chitin. In the

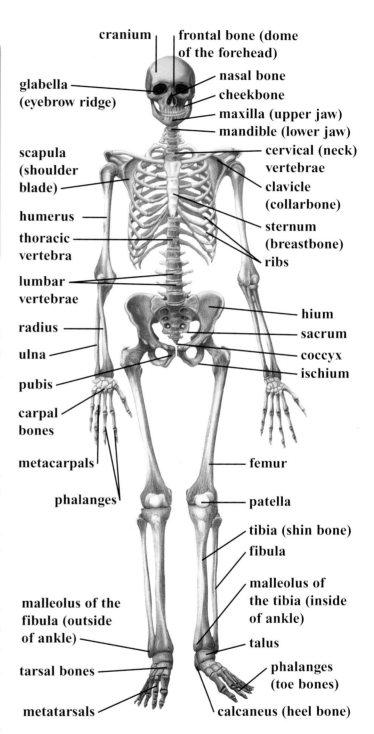

▲ The human skeleton consist of more than two hundred different bones, some of which are shown in this illustration. Most of the bones support the body and protect the soft internal organs. The largest bones are in the leg. The smallest are inside the ear. The skull, or cranium, consists of several bones that are fused into a single hollow case of bone.

its shape. Earthworms are made up of several body segments. Inside each segment is a doughnut-shaped bag of liquid. This bag is surrounded by muscles. Some muscles make the bag narrower; others make it shorter. As the bag is pulled, the volume of liquid inside stays the same size. Therefore, a narrowed bag becomes taller, while a shortened one becomes wider. Earthworms move by pushing and pulling on each of their body segments.

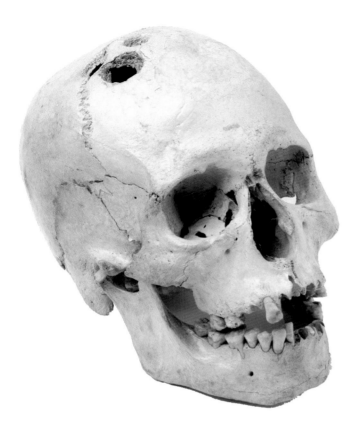

▲ *The skull holds the brain. The brain is connected to the body via the spinal cord that comes out of a hole at the base of the skull. The jaw bone is also attached to the skull.*

case of the shells of crabs and other shellfish, the chitin is strengthened with a chalky substance called calcium carbonate ($CaCO_3$). This is the same substance that gives bones their strength.

Soft or hard skeletons?
Hard shells and other skeletons also protect the body's soft internal organs from being damaged during falls or fights. For example, a person's ribcage protects their heart and lungs. However, not all skeletons are hard. Some are made of liquid.

Earthworms are an example of an animal with a liquid, or hydrostatic, skeleton. Solid substances are hard because they cannot be squeezed. The same is not true of liquids, so they can be used to give a body

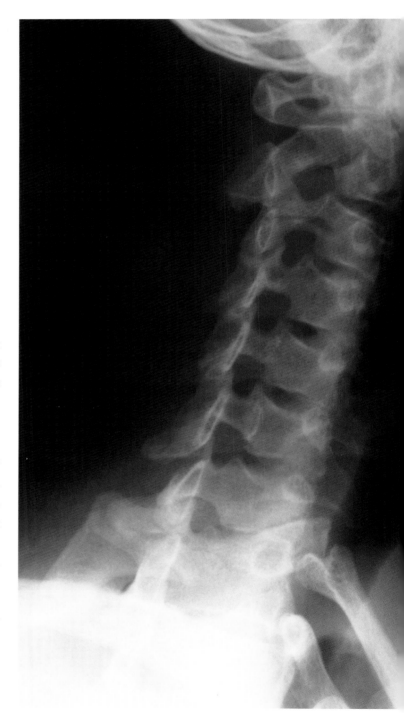

▶ *The spine, or backbone, consists of 34 separate bones, each one called a vertebra. Animals with backbones are named vertebrates for these small bones. Together, the vertebrae make a flexible column.*

1562

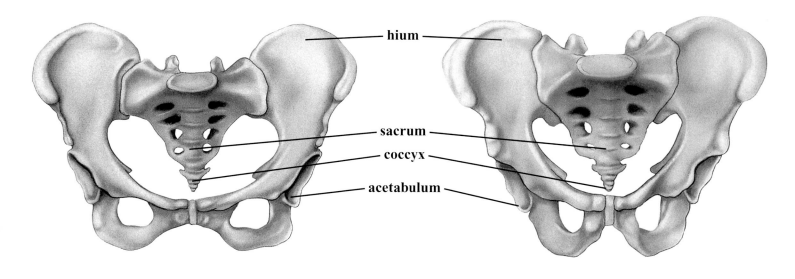

ilium

sacrum

coccyx

acetabulum

▲ *The pelvis is where the backbone joins onto the legs. Humans have an unusually shaped pelvis to help them stand upright and walk on two legs. The female pelvis (left) is wider than the male pelvis (right) to make it easier for childbirth.*

The human skeleton

Skeletons are often all that remain of dead people, and they are usually thought of as being dead. However, although the bones inside living people are hard, they are very much alive, just like any other part of the body. They have blood vessels and nerves and grow like any other body tissue. A newborn baby boy is less than 2 feet (60 centimeters) long. By the time he is an adult, he may be 6 feet (1.8 meters) tall or more. When bones crack or break in half, they knit together again.

There are 206 bones in the human body. They have a hard outer layer and a soft middle, called the marrow. Bones are as strong and tough as concrete. They can support great weights without breaking.

The bones are joined by bands of cartilage, called ligaments. These allow the bones to move, forming a joint. There are soft fat pads on the end of each bone, so they do not grind against each other as they move. Muscles pull on the bones to make them move. Muscles are attached to the bones by strong cords, called tendons.

A common disease that affects bones is arthritis. This painful complaint is caused when joints become stiff and inflamed.

DID YOU KNOW?

Fossil skulls tell us much about how living things, including humans, developed on Earth. The cranium (brain cavity) indicates brain size, while the jaws and teeth reveal what the creatures may have eaten.

Most scientists believe that the first hominid (humanlike animal) was *Australopithecus*, whose fossil remains date back about 4 million years. The oldest australopithecine fossil was found in Ethiopia; others have been located in southern Africa. Scientists think Africa was the center of human evolution.

Larger brains were important for the way human ancestors developed. However, people with big heads are not necessarily smarter than people with smaller ones. More important is the way the nerves and brain centers are organized, and it is not possible to learn anything about this from fossil skulls.

In 2004, scientists found the skeletons of tiny hominids. Named *Homo floresienses*, these little people were no more than 3⅓ feet (1 meter) high. They lived on the island of Flores in Indonesia until about 13,000 years ago.

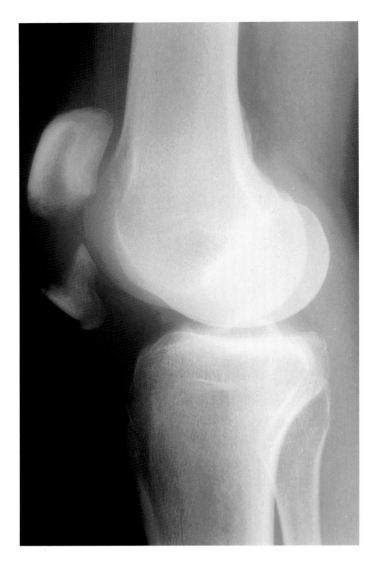

◄ The bones inside the knee are shown in this X-ray image. The thighbone and shinbone are connected to the knee by stretchy bands, called ligaments, that do not show up in X-ray images.

The ribcage is made up of the curved ribs, the spinal column at the back, and the breastbone (sternum) down the front. This framework of bone protects the soft tissues of the heart and lungs.

Arms and legs

The arms are joined to the spinal column by the scapula (shoulder blade) and the clavicle (collarbone). The big bone of the upper arm is called the humerus, and this is joined at the elbow to the two bones of the forearm, the radius and the ulna. The hand consists of a large number of small bones. The bones in the hands are shaped for picking up and handling objects.

The legs are attached to the spine by the pelvic girdle. The femur (the thighbone) is the biggest bone in the body. There are two bones in the lower leg, the tibia (shinbone) and the thinner fibula. The feet, like the hands, consist of several small bones, which form a platform for walking and running.

Babies' bones

A newborn baby has 350 bones, but as he or she grows, some of them fuse. The skeleton is complete by the time a person is about 20 years old, at which time he or she will have 206 bones. A baby's head is also much bigger in proportion to his or her body compared to an adult. When the baby is born, the head is the same length as the chest.

Broken bones

When a bone breaks, this is called a fracture. Some fractures are much more serious than others because the broken bone ends can damage other parts of the body, such as blood vessels and nerves. Fractures are usually treated by keeping the broken parts together inside a plaster cast or sling. This enables the broken bones to knit back together.

Parts of the skeleton

The skeleton is a framework on which the other parts of the body are hung and supported. Each section of the skeleton does a particular job. The skull protects the brain, the eyes, and the ears. The upper teeth are also attached to the skull. (The lower ones are embedded in the jawbone.) There are holes in the skull for the eyes, ears, and spinal cord. The spinal cord connects the brain to the rest of the body.

The backbone (spine) is made up of a chain of small bones called vertebrae. Between the vertebrae are flat discs of tough cartilage. These discs act as cushions between the vertebrae. Because the backbone consists of a number of smaller bones, it can bend in all directions. The bottom vertebra is called the coccyx, or tailbone. In most vertebrates, the coccyx is connected to a tail.

See also: DENTISTRY • NERVOUS SYSTEM

Skin

The skin is the outer covering of the human body. It is soft and flexible, but it is also strong enough to keep the internal organs safe. It stops dirt from getting inside the body and prevents the blood and all the other parts from spilling out.

The skin does more than just protect the body from attack by bacteria and other agents of disease. It is a living part of the human body. It also helps control body temperature, so that people can live in cold or hot climates while the body stays at more or less the same temperature. (A healthy person has a temperature of about 98°F or 37°C.)

Skin protects people from the harmful rays in sunlight by making a dark-colored chemical that absorbs the rays and stops them from damaging cells. Skin also automatically makes itself thicker and harder wherever people use it most, such as the palms of the hands and the soles of the feet.

The makeup of skin

Skin consists of two layers. The outer layer is called the epidermis and is made of layers of cells. The cells in each layer grow from the germinal (growth) layer at the bottom of the epidermis. Each time a layer is produced, it pushes the older layers outward. As the layer moves nearer the surface of the body, the cells become flatter and start to die. By the time they reach the outside of the body, all the cells in a layer have died, and they are coated in a waxy substance called keratin. This makes the dead cells tough but flexible (able to bend and stretch), which is ideal for forming a protective surface.

A skin cell takes about three or four weeks to reach the surface. It does not stay there long. People lose skin cells all the time. They rub off on clothes

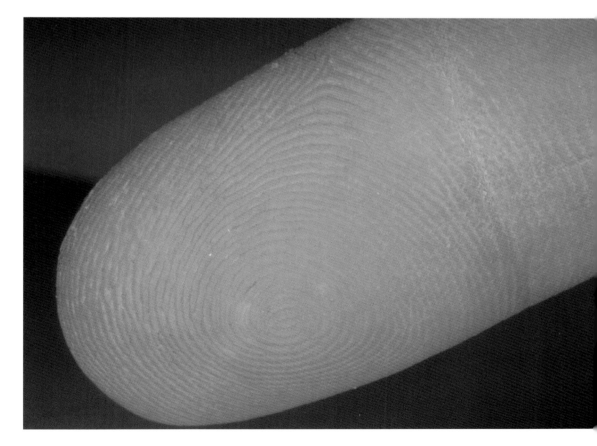

▶ A person's palm and fingertips are hairless. This makes them more sensitive to touch. The skin of the hand and fingers is also covered in ridges of loose skin. These ridges help the hand grip objects. The pattern of the ridges on each fingertip is unique. When people touch objects, they leave prints of their fingertips. Police can use the fingerprints to identify the people present at a crime scene.

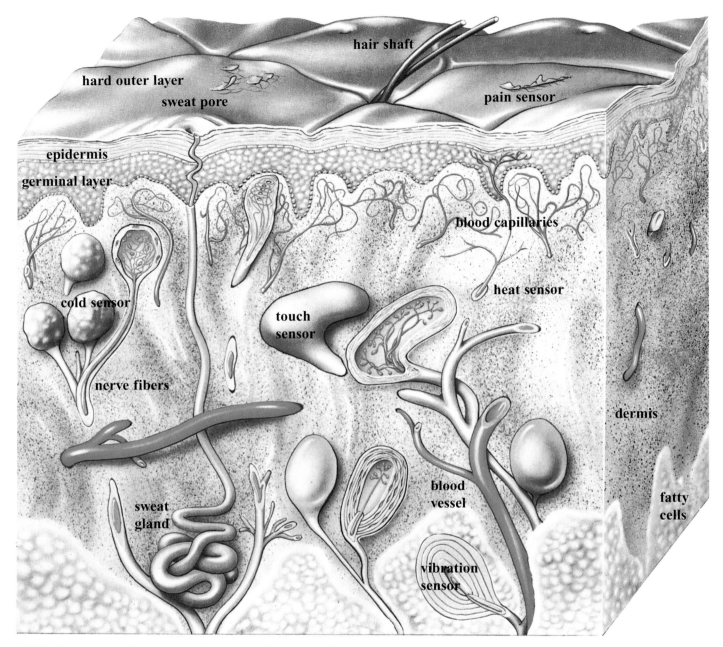

hair shaft

hard outer layer
sweat pore

pain sensor

epidermis

germinal layer

blood capillaries

cold sensor

touch
sensor

heat sensor

nerve fibers

dermis

sweat
gland

blood
vessel

fatty
cells

vibration
sensor

▲ This illustration shows an enlarged section through human skin. The epidermis (outer skin) is produced by the germinal layer. Each layer is pushed outward by the newer layers growing beneath. By the time a layer reaches the epidermis, its cells are dead, and they form a hard layer to protect the living cells below. The dead cells are constantly falling away (forming dust), and cells from below take their place. The dermis (inner skin) contains many nerve endings, glands, and blood vessels. It is much thicker than the epidermis.

▶ This illustration of a slice through a piece of skin shows a growing hair. The hair grows out of a follicle (root). The hair is oiled to slide easily through the skin, and this oil, or sebum, is made by the sebaceous gland.

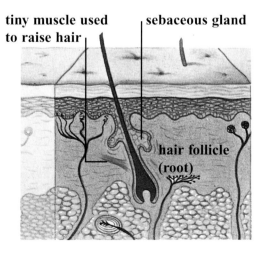

tiny muscle used
to raise hair

sebaceous gland

hair follicle
(root)

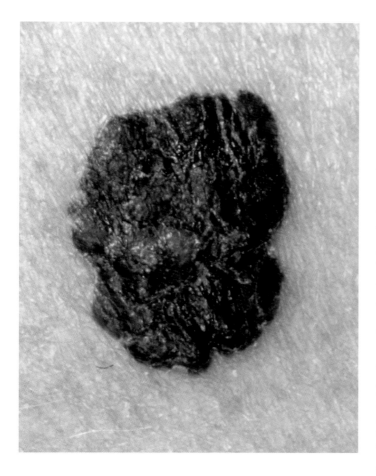

◄ *Dark spots on the skin are called moles. Most are harmless. They form when the cells that produce skin pigment grow too fast. On rare occasions, moles may start growing bigger or become sore and begin to bleed. If they are not removed or treated, these moles may turn into damaging cancers.*

Some of the ducts in the dermis are tiny blood vessels, called capillaries, that supply skin cells with oxygen and nutrients. The blood vessels also help control body temperature. When the body is hot, the capillaries widen to let more blood into the skin. This may make the skin become red. Since this blood is closer to the outside, it loses heat and the body cools down. When it is cold, the blood vessels become narrower, and the blood cannot reach the surface, which helps the body retain heat.

Animals keep warm by fluffing out their fur. This traps a layer of warm air close to their bodies. The fur hairs normally lie flat along the skin. However, they can be raised by tiny muscles near the roots. People have less hairs on the skin, but they are still used in the same way. Goosebumps on the skin are caused by the muscles in the dermis tightening to raise the hairs.

or on anything people touch. They also come off when people wash their hands and face. These lost skin cells make up a large part of the dust that gathers inside houses. Some parts of the body, like the hands, lose skin more quickly, but the whole body surface is slowly replaced over several months.

The epidermis has ducts (tubes) running through it. Many of these open onto the surface as pores. Some ducts are for hairs to grow though. Others carry sweat up to the surface. Sweat is produced by glands in the dermis. It is produced when the body is hot. The sweat evaporates from the skin and cools the body down.

The dermis

Under the epidermis is another layer, called the dermis, which is full of ducts and glands. The skin is an important sense organ. It is used to touch objects, and it can sense the temperature outside the body. The sensors that detect heat, cold, and pressure on the skin are located mainly in the dermis. Nerves connect these sensors to the brain.

Skin color

In the lowest layer of the epidermis are cells that make a dark pigment (coloring substance) called melanin. This substance is dark because it absorbs light. (Pale things reflect light.) It is used to trap harmful rays in sunlight before they reach the lower layers in the skin. A dark-skinned person produces more melanin than a light-skinned person.

Burn treatment

When skin is badly burned, the body loses a lot of liquid through the burned area. The skin cannot grow back, so doctors graft some of the victim's healthy skin over the burn. If too much of a person's skin has been burned, doctors can grow new skin for him or her in a laboratory.

See also: BRAIN • CELL • CIRCULATORY SYSTEM • EXOCRINE SYSTEM • TOUCH

Skyscraper

Skyscrapers are very tall, modern buildings found mostly in large cities to house people and businesses. The great size and weight of these massive structures make them complicated to design and build, but architects are constantly striving to make them bigger and taller.

People have been constructing tall buildings for centuries. Long before the relatively recent appearance of the skyscraper, huge constructions were soaring into the sky in many parts of the world. Most of these early tall buildings were temples or tombs, designed to connect humans with the heavens.

The earliest tall buildings were ziggurats, a form of temple common to the Sumerians, Babylonians, and Assyrians who lived in present-day Iraq. The earliest examples of ziggurats date from before 3000 BCE, predating the famous pyramids of Egypt. The pyramids were built between about 2500 BCE and 1500 BCE.

Later centuries saw the construction of large buildings in many other parts of the world, notably the great cathedrals of Europe built during the Middle Ages.

Many of these early buildings were tall, but they were not designed to be used in the same way as functional buildings such as skyscrapers. Tombs, such as pyramids, had little internal space compared with their massive walls, so their height could be easily supported. To build skyscrapers this way would be impractical because they need large amounts of interior space. Conversely, cathedrals were ingeniously designed to enclose large spaces, but they contain only a ground floor. Their foundations do not have to support additional, higher floors, or stories, as do skyscrapers.

The first skyscrapers

The development of the skyscraper began in the United States in the late nineteenth century. Architects were beginning to discover the limitations of traditional building techniques. Building

▼ *Skyscrapers dominate Chicago's cityscape and have come to dominate many other city skylines. Skyscrapers provide valuable space in crowded urban centers.*

▶ *The Petronas Towers in Kuala Lumpur, Malaysia, are some of the tallest skyscrapers in the world. Many skyscrapers are angular and look very similar, but the design of these towers deliberately reflects local, traditional architecture.*

construction at the time relied on the idea of the load-bearing wall. The walls of a building provided the barrier between inside and outside, and also transmitted the building's weight to the ground. The taller and heavier a building became, the thicker the walls had to be to support the weight. This method of construction severely restricted the height of conventional buildings.

Aside from the construction difficulties of very tall buildings, another problem was that of access. The more stories that a building had, the more stairs that people had to travel up and down. For this reason, buildings of many more than five floors were impractical as well as difficult to construct.

In the United States at this time, however, there was a growing social and economic pressure for taller buildings. New York and Chicago in particular were becoming overcrowded, and, with the formation of large corporations, individual companies wanted to house all their employees in one building. It was these two factors that were the driving forces behind the development of the skyscraper. Two significant developments made higher buildings possible—the elevator and mass-produced steel.

The elevator

The idea of an elevator had been around for a long time, but the first examples were dangerous devices, and the public distrusted them. In 1852 U.S. inventor Elisha Otis (1811–1861) invented the "safety elevator." This invention worked in almost the same way as other elevators, with a motor raising and lowering an elevator car with the help of a system of cables, pulleys, and counterweights. However, a crucial difference in Otis's design was the addition of a safety brake. Any failure in the elevator system caused the brake to operate and clamp the elevator in place. So, for the first time, people trusted elevators enough to use them.

The steel age

The second invention that made the development of the skyscraper possible was the mass production of structural steel, which made new methods of construction available. U.S. architect William Jenny (1832–1907) was the first to realize that a steel frame, rather than bricks and mortar, could be used to carry a building's weight to the ground. The advantage of steel was that it was stronger and lighter than previous materials.

The first tall buildings disguised their structures behind traditional facades. In the early twentieth century, however, architects started to recognize the freedom the new building techniques gave them. New York's 792-foot (241-meter) Woolworth Building, built between 1910 and 1913, is a key building of this period, and it is often called the first skyscraper. The Woolworth Building pioneered many important skyscraper construction methods, including the principle of using deep-foundation piles. It also solved many of the problems of supplying services, such as heating, electricity, and sanitation, to the upper levels of the building.

Types of construction

As skyscrapers have risen in height, the way they are built has changed. Continuing developments in engineering and building materials during the twentieth and twenty-first centuries also improved the techniques for building skyscrapers. There are now four principle construction methods that are widely used.

The simplest method is core-wall construction, which relies on the principle of the cantilever (a projecting beam supported at one end). The core of the skyscraper is a hollow square tube made from concrete reinforced with steel rods. With its solid walls, this construction is rigid. Cantilever beams are anchored in the core wall and are made of prestressed concrete, which increases the weight they can support. The cantilevers are extended from the core in every direction, resulting in a cylindrical or polygonal (many-sided) building. A lightweight concrete floor is laid on top of the cantilevers. Where necessary, steel columns transfer weight down the outer ends of the cantilevers to the ground, adding to the building's stability. An exterior curtain wall, usually made of glass, is suspended from the floors.

Core-wall construction is a popular method of construction for small skyscrapers. There is an upper limit to the height of the building a core-wall construction can support, so for buildings of more than 20 stories, other construction methods are used.

A second method of construction is the framed-tube method. It is based on steel components called trees. The trees are stacked and then linked together to form a framework of beams and columns that run close to the perimeter of the building. The trees are then anchored to the ground by deep piles. Steel beams are fixed to the trees, crisscrossing the building and supporting corrugated metal floors overlaid with concrete. The outsides of the trees support a glass curtain wall.

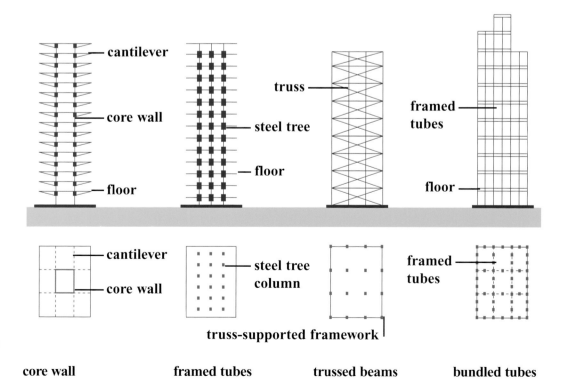

▶ These diagrams illustrate the four main types of skyscraper construction. Cross-sections of each elevation show (in red) where the main supports for different structures are located.

core wall   framed tubes   trussed beams   bundled tubes

◀ *At 1,284 feet (468 meters) high, the Shanghai Oriental Pearl Tower is one of the highest towers in the world and higher than most skyscrapers. Towers use different construction methods than skyscrapers.*

To resolve the problem of the increasing number of columns required for taller buildings, another construction method uses a system of trusses to transfer the main forces in a building. Trusses are long, diagonal beams that cross each wall. Because the trusses transmit most of the building's weight to the ground, they must be well anchored. A horizontal and vertical framework extends from the trusses to make the building's walls, and this supports the beams and curtain wall just as in a framed-tube building.

The very tallest buildings in the world use bundled tube construction. This method involves building with a series of framed tubes arranged alongside and on top of each other. Bundled tubes are very stable, and because weight is transmitted down the internal frames, the number of columns on each frame can be reduced.

Wind and earthquakes

Buildings must not only be strong enough to stand once they are built, they must also be able to resist extreme weather and geological conditions. If a building is to be built in an area where there are frequent earthquakes or high winds, the architects must ensure that the building will be strong enough to withstand any of these forces. Some skyscrapers in vulnerable areas have something called a "tuned-mass damper" inside them. This device prevents the building from swaying too much. A huge weight is placed toward the top of the building. Computers measure the amount of sway and then move the weight (damper) in the opposite direction to counterbalance the building. Engineers have developed rubber bearings for the foundations of skyscrapers in earthquake-prone regions. They help the building to absorb (soak up) the effects of Earth's movements and to remain upright.

With a framed-tube building, it is the network of columns formed by the trees that supports the structure. Because the tube is a flexible structure, it bends slightly in the wind, making it more resistant to sudden winds than a completely rigid building. The forces created by expansion and compression of opposite sides of the tube act to right the building. This construction has particular advantages because it is not subject to the usual height limitations. To build a higher or heavier building, it is simply necessary to increase the number or width of the load-bearing columns.

See also: ARCHITECTURE • BUILDING TECHNIQUES

Sleep and dreams

People spend about one-third of their lives asleep. Sleep is a vital way for the body to replenish the energy used up during the day. Only very recently have scientists begun to find out what exactly sleep is and what happens in the brain when people are asleep.

When a person is asleep, his or her body continues to function normally—the lungs continue to draw in oxygen from the air, the heart pumps blood around the body, and cells continue to metabolize food to make energy for the body. People also toss and turn in bed, and sometimes even talk or walk in their sleep. So the brain does not shut down completely when a person is asleep. It is still in control of the body and never stops working. In fact, some parts of the brain are very active during sleep.

Stages of sleep

Scientists have identified four distinct stages of sleep by measuring the electrical activity in the brain using an electroencephalograph (EEG). The EEG detects tiny electrical currents in the brain using electrodes placed on the head. When a person is awake, the EEG records a distinctive, rapid pattern of brain waves (the shapes of electrical

▼ *Newborn babies sleep for up to 17 hours every day, waking and sleeping on roughly a 90-minute cycle.*

STAGES OF SLEEP

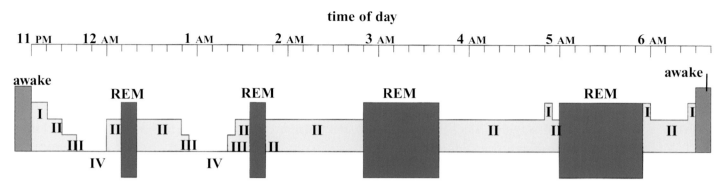

▲ *This illustration shows the likely movement between the different stages of sleep during a normal sleep cycle.*

waves in the brain), called the alpha rhythm. As the person gets drowsier, his or her brain waves become less active, slower, and more regular.

On average, it takes a person about 15 minutes to fall asleep. First, the person enters a period of light sleep, called stage I sleep. The EEG records a characteristic wave pattern, called a theta wave, that follows a period of between four to eight cycles every second. Soon after, the person enters stage II sleep, which is characterized by periodic short bursts of brain waves. Stage III sleep follows, which reverts back to the characteristic theta pattern, but with a period of between two and four cycles every second. Finally, the person will enter stage IV sleep,

BRAIN WAVE PATTERNS

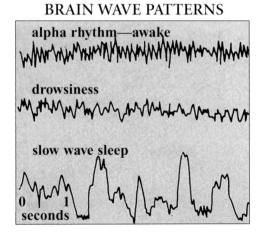

▲ *Brain waves can be recorded using an electroencephalograph (EEG). The electrical activity in the brain is picked up by wires placed on the scalp. The brain produces different wave patterns during the different stages of sleep.*

▶ *The sleep/awake center in the brain takes signals from the body and from the rest of the brain. The brain then decides whether or not to go to sleep. Pain or cold may keep people awake. Some drugs, warmth, or even boredom can send people to sleep.*

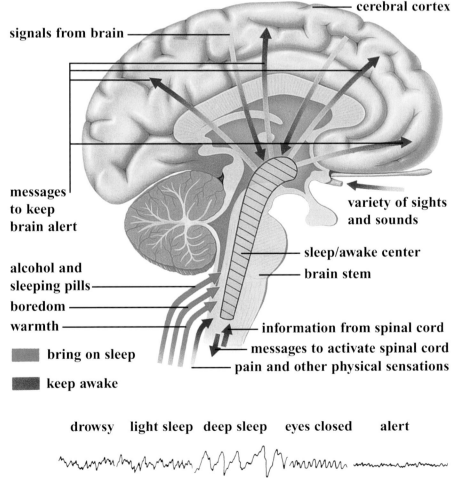

which also features the theta wave pattern but at a much lower frequency—between a half to two cycles per second. Stage IV sleep is the deepest sleep and usually occurs about 30 minutes after a person falls asleep. If a person is awakened during stage IV sleep, he or she will feel very tired and will need a few minutes to become fully alert again.

After about an hour of stage IV sleep, the sleeper will slowly move back through the stages to stage I. The sleep cycle then repeats one or two times through to stage III or stage IV sleep. For the rest of the night, the sleeper will spend most of the time moving between stage I and stage II sleep.

REM sleep

Stage I sleep changes in an important way after the first descent into stage IV. Each time the sleeper subsequently enters stage I sleep, the active brain wave pattern recorded on the EEG is accompanied by rapid eye movement (REM). People move between periods of REM and non-REM sleep during the night in 90-minute cycles. REM sleep is usually accompanied by dreams.

The body clock

The internal body clock is situated in the brain stem, which is a long, narrow section at the bottom of the brain. It is responsible for the 24-hour cycle of sleeping and waking, as well as variations in body temperature. This cycle is called the circadian rhythm. For most people, body temperature and alertness are at their highest in the morning, they gradually decrease toward the evening, reaching their lowest point during deep stage IV sleep.

How much the body relies on the internal body clock can be illustrated when airline passengers fly through different time zones. Some people arrive at their destination but feel like they want to go to sleep. It may be mid-afternoon at their destination, but the brain thinks it is time to sleep because it has not adjusted to the different time zone. This effect is known as jet lag.

Dreams

Everyone appears to dream during REM sleep, although not everyone remembers his or her dreams. Those dreams that are remembered

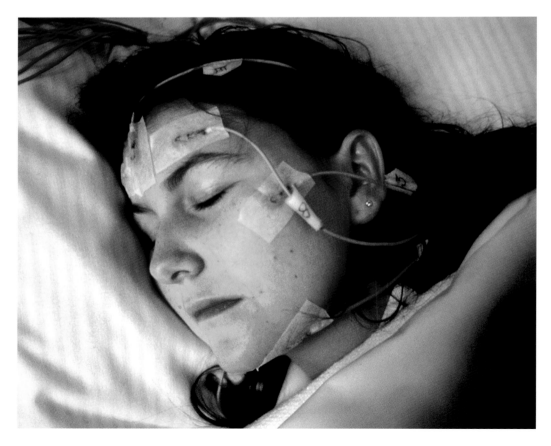

◀ *Electrodes placed on the scalp of this woman pick up electrical activity in the brain. The wires are attached to an electroencephalograph (EEG), which displays the brain activity as distinctive wave patterns.*

▶ *Stimulant drugs such as caffeine in coffee, tea, and cola drinks keep people awake. Some people are more sensitive to the effects of caffeine than others. One person may be able to drink a dozen cups of tea with little effect on his or her sleep, while another person will stay awake all night after only one cup of coffee.*

probably occurred during the last cycle of REM sleep before waking. Dreaming seems to be a vital part of the sleep cycle. A person who is prevented from dreaming for even a few nights may become nervous and irritable.

Scientists cannot agree on exactly how dreaming helps people relax. Scientists try to learn about dreams by using volunteers. These people go to sleep in research clinics where the scientists can watch how they sleep, often using cameras to check on the sleeper's movements.

Some believe that sleep gives the brain a chance to sweep away all the useless thoughts left over from the day. In this way, people may literally "dream away" problems as they sleep. Others think that because the brain is active even when people are asleep, it is just working away on its own, using any thoughts and feelings that it can find. It is the brain's way of keeping itself amused until the person wakes up and takes control of the mind and body again.

People sometimes find that they go to sleep thinking about a problem and wake up to find that their brains have solved it while they slept. Much more research is needed before scientists can be sure how dreams really work.

Too much or too little

Various disorders interfere with sleep. Narcolepsy is a sleep disorder that makes people fall asleep without warning at any time of the day. The exact causes of narcolepsy are not fully understood, but the condition can be treated using stimulants.

Everyone experiences some form of insomnia, or lack of sleep, during their lives. There are two main forms of insomnia—the inability to fall asleep and the tendency to wake up and then be unable to fall back to sleep. Insomnia has many causes, ranging from anxiety and stress to the excessive consumption of caffeine and other stimulants.

Many people who suffer from sleep deprivation turn to sleeping pills to help them sleep. However, it has been found that some drugs will give patients only a deep sleep. These drugs may prevent REM sleep and therefore stop the patient from dreaming. Because dreaming is vital for healthy sleep, these drugs may be harmful if taken for too long. Another problem with sleeping pills is that many people gradually require larger doses to get them to sleep. Eventually, they may become addicted to them and may not be able to sleep without them.

See also: BIORHYTHM • BRAIN • EYE AND VISION • MUSCULAR SYSTEM • NERVOUS SYSTEM

Smell

Many people regard smell as the least important of the human senses, but it is very significant. Within three days of birth, a human baby can recognize the smell of his or her mother. People use odors to appreciate the taste of food, and smell can also warn against certain dangerous situations. Many scientists have tried to understand how people tell different smells apart, but the process is still poorly understood.

▲ The fragrant smell of garden flowers is caused by organic molecules called esters evaporating from the flowers and floating through the air into the nose.

Animals use their sense of smell to provide them with information about their surroundings. For example, the sense of smell can help a lion to locate an antelope, and it can warn the antelope that a lion is approaching. Smell also plays a part in sexual attraction in most animals.

People no longer rely on the sense of smell to find food or a sexual partner or to avoid getting eaten by a predator. As a result, people have a limited sense of smell compared to most other animals. Dogs, for example, can detect some odors that are far too faint for people to notice.

How smell works

When a person smells a fragrant perfume or spicy food, he or she is detecting gas molecules given off by the perfume or the food. These gas molecules are detected by the nose. Odors are taken into the nose when people breathe. The inside of the nose is covered with a thin layer of moist tissue, called a mucous membrane, which is filled with many tiny blood vessels and sensitive nerves.

When an odor comes in contact with the mucous membrane of the nose, some of the molecules in the odor dissolve in its damp surface. The dissolved odor molecules are then picked up by hairs called olfactory (smell) cilia, which are connected to olfactory cells. When the cilia react to the odor, they activate the olfactory cells, which then send signals to a large olfactory bulb. There, the signals are collected and sorted before being sent to the brain through the olfactory nerve.

Smell, taste, and feeling

The sense of taste is closely linked to the sense of smell. People can taste the difference only between bitter, sweet, salt, and sour. Other "tastes" actually result from the sense of smell. The link between taste and smell has another effect. When people smell good food, they feel hungry. This happens automatically. The smell triggers hunger pangs in the same way as a burning match touching a finger triggers the reflex action that makes the hand pull away from the match.

Smell also triggers strong memories and emotions, because the olfactory bulb is linked to the brain's limbic system (the source of emotions) and the hippocampus (the memory center).

The science of smell

Scientists have been able to figure out roughly how the sense of smell works, but the exact science of smell is not fully understood. The main problem is how people can tell so many different smells apart. People can correctly name hundreds of objects by their smell alone and can even describe a new smell by saying that it resembles another known smell. How do people do this so easily and quickly?

Just as there are only four basic tastes, so there are only six basic odors: spicy, fruity, floral, resinous, foul, and burned. Different amounts of these basic smells make up all the odors it is possible to smell.

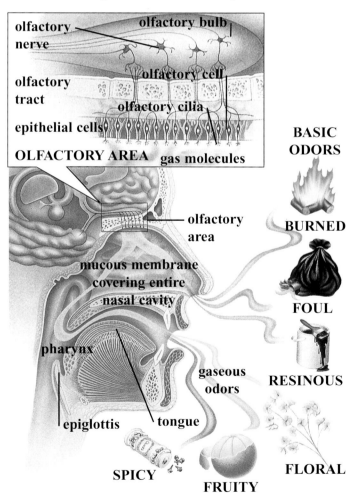

OLFACTORY AREA

olfactory nerve
olfactory bulb
olfactory cell
olfactory tract
olfactory cilia
epithelial cells
gas molecules

olfactory area

mucous membrane covering entire nasal cavity

pharynx

gaseous odors

epiglottis   tongue

SPICY
FRUITY
FLORAL
RESINOUS
FOUL
BURNED

BASIC ODORS

▲ *Inhaled air passes into the nasal cavity, where chemicals are detected by olfactory (sensory) cells.*

Each of these basic odors is recognized in one of two different ways—either by the size and shape of the gas molecules or by the particular electrical charge of the gas molecules. For example, floral odors consist of gas molecules that are the right shape and size for particular olfactory cilia. Scientists think that these cilia then count up the number of floral gas molecules in any particular odor to interpret the smell. On the other hand, foul odors are recognized by their negative electrical charge and so are attracted only to positively charged parts of the olfactory cilia. For each smell detected, each basic odor is detected and combined to form an overall impression of the smell.

The olfactory bulb has the difficult task of taking in all the signals from the cilia and figuring out how many particles of each type of basic odor are present. This information is sent to the brain, which must then identify exactly what kind of smell it is. When it has the answer, it sends messages to other parts of the brain, so the right action can be taken. In this way, the olfactory system allows people to distinguish up to 10,000 different smells.

The olfactory cilia are highly sensitive, but they get used to a smell very quickly, and no longer respond to it. Even the odor of rotten eggs is no longer repulsive after a few minutes. This effect is called olfactory fatigue.

Disorders of smell

The sense of smell can be impaired in many ways. Temporary loss of smell (and taste) is often caused by a common cold, when the nose becomes blocked with mucus. Brain injuries, tumors, and exposure to certain chemicals, for example, those found in cigarette smoke, may cause a permanent loss of the sense of smell. Synesthesia is another extremely rare condition that can affect the sense of smell. People with synesthesia experience one sense in the form of another, for example, smells as colors or tastes as shapes. Scientists do not fully understand the mechanisms behind synesthesia.

See *also:* BRAIN • TASTE

Snow and frost

Snow and frost are familiar sights in winter in cooler temperature zones, and also at high altitudes throughout the world. Snow is a mass of tiny ice crystals. The crystal surface of fresh snow reflects light; snow therefore looks white. Frost is frozen moisture formed either from dew or from water vapor condensed directly from the air into ice crystals.

All air contains moisture in the form of water vapor, most of which has come from the oceans. When moist air rises, it gradually becomes cooler. Cold air cannot hold as much water vapor as warm air. When the air reaches the dew point, it is saturated, which means that the air is holding all the water vapor it can at that temperature.

Further cooling beyond the dew point makes some of the water vapor condense (turn back into a liquid) around tiny bits of dust, salt, and other particles in the air. Condensation produces tiny water droplets, so light that they hang in the air. Large amounts of these droplets form clouds.

In warm climates, water droplets often merge inside clouds until they become large enough to fall as raindrops. In cool climates, most clouds have a temperature below the freezing point of water (32°F or 0°C). These clouds consist of tiny crystals of ice and supercooled water droplets. Supercooled droplets remain as a liquid even though their temperature is well below the freezing point, often as low as 5°F (−15°C). In these clouds, the supercooled droplets freeze when they touch ice crystals. As a result, the ice crystals grow until they become so heavy that they fall to the ground.

If the temperature near the ground is below the freezing point, the crystals fall as snow. If the temperature is slightly above the freezing point, some flakes melt and fall as sleet (a mixture of snow and rain). If the temperature of the air is more than about 39°F (4°C), however, all the snowflakes melt, and they fall as raindrops.

Shapes and sizes

Snowflakes form delicate crystals, all of which have six sides but with an unlimited number of shapes. Some are flat plates; others look like columns. The shape a crystal takes depends on many factors, including air temperature and humidity.

▶ *A busy street is covered with ice following a storm in Montreal, Canada. Snow and ice settle on the ground when the air temperature is below the freezing point of water (32°F or 0°C).*

► *Skiing is a popular leisure pursuit for many people. By spreading the weight of the body over the wide surface area of the skis, a skier can slide over the snow without sinking into it.*

▼ *This light micrograph reveals the hexagonal center of a snowflake. No two snowflakes are identical because each experiences a wide range of conditions as it forms inside a cloud.*

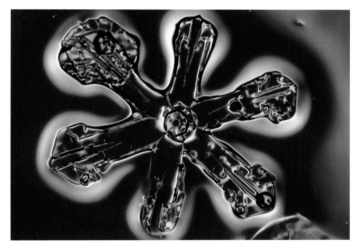

of the snow and record the level of the water because the amount of water in snow can vary greatly. About 6 inches (15 centimeters) of wet snow or 30 inches (76 centimeters) of dry snow might both be equal to 1 inch (2.5 centimeters) of rainfall.

Snowstorms

Blizzards are storms in which powdery snow is blown about by high winds. They reduce visibility to almost zero. In 1996, blizzards paralyzed the East Coast of the United States, causing $3 billion in damage and killing 187 people.

Frost

There are three kinds of frost. Hoar frost is the delicate pattern of crystallized ice that forms on windows. Glazed frost forms when rain falls on surfaces that are well below the freezing point. The surfaces are then coated with ice, which is often very thick. Glazed frost on telegraph and telephone wires may become so heavy that it pulls down the wires. Rime forms when supercooled water droplets freeze after they touch cold objects. Rime looks like icing around the edges of petals and leaves and only occurs when the temperatures are very low.

Hailstones are lumps of ice formed when there are strong upcurrents of air within a cloud. The upcurrents often sweep the raindrops up to great heights, where it is well below the freezing point. The raindrops then freeze into hard pellets of ice, which grow in size as they are coated with water vapor. Finally, they become so heavy that they fall, no matter how strong the upcurrents of air may be.

The largest hailstone ever recorded fell in Bangladesh in 1986. It weighed more than 2 pounds (1 kilogram). The hailstorm reportedly killed more than 90 people.

The world's greatest snowfall in a year was a little more than 1,224 inches (3,110 centimeters) at Paradise, Mount Rainier, Washington, between 1971 and 1972. Scientists at weather stations melt samples

See also: CLOUD • CRYSTAL • RAIN AND RAINFALL • TEMPERATURE • WEATHER SYSTEM

Soap and detergent

Soap has been used as a cleaning agent for about five thousand years. Recently, scientists have discovered how to make new kinds of detergents. Ideal for cleaning, soap and detergents have many other uses.

Water alone is not a good cleaning agent because it does not make things very wet. On many surfaces, such as a piece of dry cloth, water forms tiny droplets on some areas but leaves other areas completely dry. The water clings together, as if it were covered by a film. This property is called surface tension. If a glass is filled with water, the water can bulge over the brim without spilling. The strength of this surface tension can be observed by placing a needle on a paper towel and floating it in a bowl of water. As the paper sinks, the needle floats on the surface, held up by the tension.

For water to flow more freely and clean objects thoroughly, the surface tension must be broken down. This is done by adding chemicals called surface active agents (surfactants) to the water.

Making water "wetter"

Detergents are surfactants. They consist of molecules with hydrophilic (water-attracting) heads and hydrophobic (water-repelling) tails. When mixed with water, the hydrophobic tails of the detergent molecules break through the surface layer of water molecules. This disrupts the surface tension of the water, making it "wetter."

When an item is being cleaned, the hydrophobic tails of the detergent molecules attach themselves to particles of dirt and grease. If the item being cleaned is then stirred or shaken, it helps the

▼ *Surgeons "scrub up" with an iodine-based detergent called E-Z Scrub. The iodine in the detergent kills any bacteria on the skin and therefore minimizes the risk of infection during the surgery.*

detergent dislodge the grease particles. Covered in surfactant, the minute droplets of grease become scattered throughout the water as an emulsion and can be rinsed away.

If a detergent is too weak, it will not clean very well. The detergent must be strong enough to form micelles—groupings of molecules with their hydrophilic heads pointing outward.

Soap manufacture

The first soap was made by boiling animal fats and wood ash in a kettle of water. The fats released acids that reacted with the alkali in the wood ash. The result was soap and a syrupy liquid called glycerin, which is used as a solvent and in lotions and explosives. This process, called saponification, is still used. Vegetable or animal fats, such as coconut oil or tallow, are boiled in an alkali such as caustic soda (sodium hydroxide; NaOH) or caustic potash (potassium hydroxide; KOH). Although the traditional method of boiling in batches is still used, modern kettles are made of steel and stand three stories high. They can hold 100,000 pounds (45,000 kilograms) of mixture.

To separate the soap from the glycerin, hot brine (a solution of sodium hydroxide; NaOH) is boiled with the mixture. Soap does not dissolve in the brine, but glycerin does. So while the soap forms into a sticky mass, the glycerin sinks to the bottom of the kettle. This bottom layer, called spent lye, can then be tapped off.

The sticky mass of soap, called the curd, must be processed further to purify it. First, a strong alkali is added to the mixture. The last step, called pitching or fitting, involves boiling the mixture with water. When it settles, there is a top layer of neat or kettle soap, consisting of 70 percent soap and 30 percent water. The lower layer, called nigre, consists of dirt, water, and up to 40 percent soap. The neat soap is skimmed off while it is still warm, and the nigre is further purified to extract more soap.

Kettle-batch production takes about a week from start to finish, so large-scale manufacturers prefer to use a continuous method. This speeds up the chemical changes by heating the mixture to a high

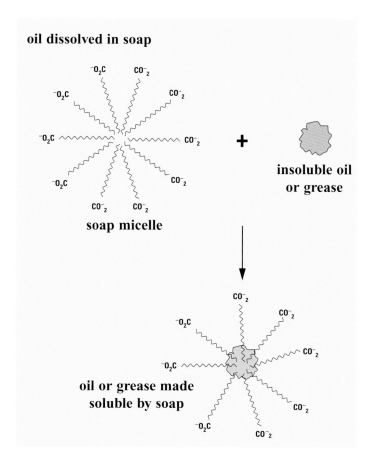

▲ A soap micelle, consisting of charged polar groups and hydrocarbon chains, surrounds a deposit of grease or oil and removes it from the water.

temperature and placing it under large pressures. A continuous stream of fat and caustic soda is fed through pumps into a pressurized column. The hot liquid is tapped off and then mixed and cooled.

Another common method of soap manufacture is called continuous hydrolysis. Hydrolysis is a way of breaking up chemical compounds by adding water to them. In the case of soap manufacture, hot fats and a catalyst (a substance that speeds up a chemical reaction) are fed into the bottom of a tall, steel column. Hot water is fed in at the top of the column. At a temperature of about 446°F (230°C) and a pressure of 569 pounds per square inch (40 kilograms per square centimeter), the fats are broken down into fatty acids and glycerin. The glycerin is tapped off from the bottom of the column, and the fatty acids are drawn off from the top. The fatty acids are then purified in a vacuum and treated with an alkali to form neat soap.

Additives and finishing

In a process called crutching, many different additives (extra ingredients) are mixed into the hot, liquid soap. Some additives improve the cleansing action of the soap. For example, abrasives—tiny particles of pumice, sand, or talc—are added to cleaners that are designed to clean heavily soiled items. The gritty action of the abrasives rubs off the dirt. Bleach and many dyes are added to make fabrics reflect light and look brighter and cleaner. Other additives include antiseptics to kill bacteria and preservatives such as sodium silicate.

The hot, liquid soap is then treated further to make the finished product. Hard, coarse soaps are produced by spray drying and pressing into bars, until the water content is about 28 percent of the weight of the soap. High-quality, perfumed bath soaps are heated after drying until their water content is reduced to around 10 percent. The ribbons of soap are fed into a machine called a plodder, which squeezes them into shape so that they can be cut into bars, stamped, and wrapped.

Soap flakes are ideal for delicate fabrics. Their large surface area and light weight makes them dissolve easily and form suds quickly. They are made by spreading hot, liquid soap over a rotating, water-cooled drum. The soap dries into thin ribbons, which then pass into a drying chamber until their water content is about 7 percent. The soap is then rolled out, cut into flakes, and packed.

Soap powder—the form of soap most suitable for use in washing machines—is spray dried. So many additives are mixed in to improve its cleaning action that only about 50 percent of the final product is actually soap.

Synthetic detergents

During World War I (1914–1918), there was a shortage of fats for soap manufacture. Scientists looked for other ways of making cleaning agents and found their answer in the petrochemicals industry. Many synthetic detergents are now manufactured from petrochemicals. Most work just as well, if not better, than soapy detergents.

Synthetic detergents work in the same way as soapy detergents. The molecules of a synthetic detergent consist of a long chain of hydrophobic hydrocarbons (molecules consisting of carbon and hydrogen atoms) joined to a hydrophilic group.

If the hydrophilic group contains a negative electrical charge, the detergent is called anionic. Many modern synthetic detergents are anionic and

▶ *A worker uses an electric saw to cut solid soap into large slabs at a factory in Marseille, France.*

▲ U.S. Coast Guard and Ecuadoran workers spray a detergent to disperse an oil spill at sea near San Cristobal in the Galápagos Island chain.

are produced by a reaction between sulfuric acid (H_2SO_4) and alkylbenzenes (hydrocarbon chains attached to benzene; C_6H_6). Caustic soda is then added to produce a surfactant paste, which can be mixed with additives and spray dried. If fatty alcohols are used in place of alkylbenzenes, the resulting detergent will be very foamy.

DID YOU KNOW?

Synthetic detergents may be contributing to water pollution. One major cause for concern is the use of additives called phosphates, which are used to soften the water. Phosphates cause excessive growth of algae and other water plants, which deplete the water's oxygen supply, killing fish and other organisms. Other detergent additives, such as bleaches and enzymes, can also be harmful to the environment.

However, many washing machines now work with detergent powders that do not produce much foam. For this purpose, nonionic detergents are used, in which the hydrophilic end has no charge. Nonionic detergents are often manufactured by heating a chemical called ethylene oxide (C_2H_4O) with an alkylphenol (hydrocarbon chains attached to phenol; C_6H_6O), using an alkaline catalyst to initiate the reaction.

If there is a positive charge on the hydrophilic end, the detergent is called cationic. These detergents are poor cleaners but good wetting agents. They make fabrics soft and are widely used as fabric conditioners.

Both soapy and synthetic detergents have a wide range of applications in addition to cleaning—including jewelry polishing, oil dispersal, paint and lubricant manufacture, road surfacing, rust prevention, and surgical and medical manufacture.

See also: ABRASIVE • ACID AND ALKALI • ATOM AND MOLECULE • FAT • PRESSURE • SURFACE TENSION • WATER

Sodium

Sodium is a metal, but it is not at all like the metals used to make nails or cars. Sodium is soft enough to be cut with a knife and so light that it will float on water. But never build a boat out of sodium; it will react violently with the water and burst into flames.

When a person sprinkles salt on food, washes his or her hands with soap, or bakes a cake, substances that contain sodium are being used. Sodium is a metal, similar to aluminum, copper, and iron. Sodium has the chemical symbol Na.

Unlike aluminum, copper, and iron, people will probably not come across pure sodium outside of a chemistry laboratory. Sodium is so reactive that it combines quickly with other elements to form compounds. Compounds contain the atoms of two or more different elements. An atom is the smallest part of an element that has all the properties of that element. Each atom is less than one-millionth of an inch across.

Pure sodium can be separated out from other elements by a complicated and expensive process involving electricity. A piece of freshly cut sodium is bright and shiny with a silvery sheen. It does not stay bright for long, though. The cut surface soon tarnishes as the sodium reacts with oxygen in the air, forming sodium oxide (Na_2O). A thin, dull gray layer of this compound rapidly covers all the surfaces of the metal. Because pure sodium reacts with almost everything in the environment, it has to be stored in oil or in a tank of liquid nitrogen.

Sodium is a metal, and it shares many characteristics with other metals. Metals are substances that conduct electricity well and react with nonmetal elements to form compounds that chemists call salts. (For example, the common salt used to flavor food is a sodium compound called sodium chloride; NaCl.)

▲ Pure sodium metal reacts with the oxygen in the air very easily. If it gets wet, the sodium may explode. Therefore, scientists store lumps of sodium in thin oil to protect the metal from these reactions.

Chemical reactions

Atoms consist of three types of smaller particles. Protons and neutrons are found at the center of the atom, where they make a dense nucleus. Protons have a positive electrical charge, while neutrons have no charge at all. The third type of particle is an electron, which moves around the nucleus in a similar way to planets orbiting the Sun. Electrons are negatively charged. Because opposite charges attract each other, the electrons are held inside the atom by the pull of the protons in the nucleus. An atom always has the same number of protons as electrons. Therefore, atoms do not have an overall charge because the opposite charges of the protons and electrons cancel each other out. Sodium has 11 protons, 11 electrons, and 12 neutrons.

Chemical reactions involve atoms losing or gaining electrons. Metal elements lose electrons easily. Sodium always loses just one electron, but other metals may lose two electrons during reactions. The electron that is lost by the sodium atom is gained by a nonmetal to form a salt.

Because it has lost an electron, the sodium atom becomes a positively charged sodium ion. This is because there are now more positive protons in the sodium than negative electrons. The nonmetal that picked up the sodium's electron becomes a negative ion. The two ions will be attracted to each other because they have an opposite charge. The ions bond together into a molecule. For example, when sodium reacts with chlorine gas (Cl), electrons are exchanged to form sodium chloride.

▼ At nighttime, sidewalks are lit up by sodium vapor lamps. These produce a bright, orange-white light and are inexpensive to power. The bulbs contain neon gas and a little sodium. An electrical current is used to heat the neon gas, making it glow. This vaporizes the sodium, forming a bright light. Sometimes mercury is added to the mixture to produce even brighter light.

Electrical properties
Sodium conducts electricity because of its ability to release electrons easily. The atoms inside a block of sodium each release an electron, which form a "sea" of electrons shared by all the sodium atoms. This sea is what bonds all the atoms into a solid. It is also what makes sodium (and other metals) so good at conducting electricity. The free electrons can flow though the metal, carrying an electrical current.

Unusual for a metal
Sodium reacts like a metal and conducts electricity well, but it is unlike most other metals. Many people think metals are hard, heavy materials. However, sodium is so soft that it can be cut with a knife, which is because its atoms fill a lot of space but do not weigh very much. Scientists describe this property of sodium as having a low density. Sodium is even less dense than water and will therefore float when it is dropped in water.

◀ *Granules of sodium compounds are often mixed up with other chemicals to make fireworks. As the gunpowder explodes, it ignites the sodium compound to create a shower of orange sparks.*

Making pure sodium

The first person to make pure sodium was English scientist Humphry Davy (1778–1829). Davy was interested in the way some substances could be split into simple substances using electricity. In 1807, Davy used a powerful battery to isolate potassium metal from a liquid containing potash (potassium carbonate; K_2CO_3). A few days later, Davy isolated sodium by passing an electrical current through molten sodium chloride.

The technique that Davy used came to be called electrolysis. The electrical current reverses the chemical reaction that made the sodium chloride in the first place. It returns the lost electrons to the sodium ions, making sodium atoms. The sodium atoms gather as pure sodium metal. Pure chlorine gas is produced as the chloride ions lose electrons.

Sodium is still made using electrolysis, although the process is now much more efficient. The sodium chloride is melted down, which makes it better able to conduct electricity. A large electrical current is then passed from a rod of graphite (a form of carbon), through the liquid salt, and into a steel rod. Pure sodium gathers in a thin layer on the steel rod, while chlorine gas bubbles out of the liquid around the graphite rod. The steel rod is periodically removed, and the pure sodium is melted and tapped off.

Uses of sodium

Sodium has many uses. Sodium chloride is used to make food taste better. Eaten in small amounts, salt also helps the body stay healthy. Sodium peroxide (Na_2O_2) is used as a bleach, for example, to whiten flour. Pure sodium carries heat well, so liquid sodium is often pumped around nuclear reactors to pick up heat from one place and take it to another.

Because the atoms of sodium are large, the sea of electrons that holds them together are a long way from the nuclei of the atoms. So the forces that pull the nuclei and electrons together are weaker in sodium than the forces in most other metals. This makes it easy to move separate sodium atoms from each other—by cutting the metal or melting it. Sodium also has a low melting point compared to most other metals. It turns into a liquid when it is heated to just 206°F (97°C).

See also: ATOM AND MOLECULE • CHEMICAL REACTION • ELECTROLYSIS • METAL

Software

Airliners, automobiles, cell phones, television remote-control units, space shuttles, washing machines, and many other electronic systems depend on computer programs, or software, to function. The progress of software is as important as the progress of hardware in the history of computing and the information revolution.

▲ *A software program is a list of instructions that tells a computer what to do. The computer translates these instructions into binary code—strings of zeros and ones that can be seen on the monitor in this picture.*

The computer has revolutionized the modern world, but it does a lot more than compute. The word *compute* strictly means "calculate." The first calculating machine could do only a limited set of mathematical tasks. Modern pocket or desktop calculators can do many more types of math, but they are not computers. In principle, computers can solve any kind of mathematical problem.

In the 1970s, the computer was developed to handle other tasks in addition to mathematics. For example, it was adapted to handle typewritten text, and word processing was born. Then the computer was developed to help artists create and manipulate digital images. Now computers are used to send e-mails and to browse the Internet. While people in homes and offices use personal computers (PCs), those in businesses and universities use more powerful computers and do an even wider range of jobs. In fact, people use computers to do any type of task that involves processing large amounts of data.

To be able to perform all these different functions, the computer has to switch instantly from being used to do one thing, such as calculating a math problem, to another, such as manipulating a digital image. It does this by using different computer programs—sets of instructions that tell the computer exactly what to do. Collectively, the programs that control the computer are called software. The physical machinery of the computer is called the hardware.

Typically, software is stored on a compact disc (CD), which the computer "reads." However, it may also be downloaded from the Internet. When the software is being run, all or part of it is copied into part of the internal memory of the computer. This memory is called random-access memory (RAM), and it holds the data and instructions that the computer is working with at any moment.

Punched cards

The data and instructions for a computer have to be "written" in a form that the computer can "read." One of the earliest ways of doing this was to use punched cards—cards with holes punched in them to represent pieces of information.

Punched cards were first used for a completely different sort of machine—a mechanical loom. In the early nineteenth century, French textile manufacture Joseph-Marie Jacquard (1752–1834) devised a way of operating his looms using cards with punched holes. The holes in the cards would allow certain rods in the loom to pass through.

1587

Where there were no holes, other rods would be blocked. As a result, different colors of threads could be used from one moment to the next, and complex designs could be woven into the fabric. Changing to a different design was just a matter of switching to a different set of punched cards.

The same principle was later used in other devices, such as the player piano. This is a piano that "plays itself" as a long roll of punched paper is fed through it by a clockwork mechanism. The patterns of holes can record not only a particular piece of music, but also a particular performance. Many great pianists made player-piano rolls around 1900, before sound recording made the device obsolete. Similar rolls can still be seen operating fairground and street organs. In this case, the pattern of holes is the software, and the musical instrument is the hardware.

Punched cards and punched paper tape became an important means of putting programs and data into computers, that is, an important medium for software. The idea for this dates back to the mid-nineteenth century, when English mathematician and inventor Charles Babbage (1792–1871) invented the Analytical Engine. This general-purpose calculating machine was so ambitious that Babbage never completed it, but he planned to operate it using punched cards.

English mathematician and writer Ada Augusta King, Countess of Lovelace (1815–1852), worked closely with Babbage and published a description of the planned Analytical Engine. King gave detailed examples of procedures controlled by the punched cards, which many regard as the first examples of computer

programs. Ada, a programming language developed for the U.S. Department of Defense in 1979, was named in her honor. (A programming language is a notation that is easy for people to understand because it resembles written words or mathematical terms. However, it is also easily translated into the binary code—the strings of zeros and ones—that a computer understands.)

Punched cards were the main storage device for software until the 1970s. From the 1970s, however, magnetic tape, similar to that used in audio cassette recorders, was used to store computer software. Later, disks with magnetic coatings on their surfaces were developed, becoming the high-capacity "hard disks" that people use today. Compact discs were then adapted as memory media, and digital video discs (DVDs) are now following suit.

Programming languages

The computer revolution was made possible by advances in both hardware and software.

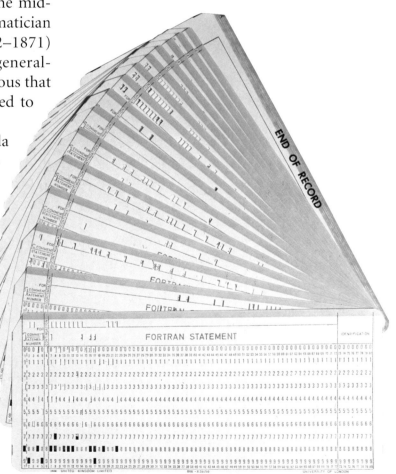

▶ *Punched cards such as these were used during the 1960s and 1970s as a common form of data input in large computer systems. Punched cards were invented by French textile manufacturer Joseph-Marie Jacquard to operate his weaving looms. The first data-processing system using punched cards was developed by U.S. inventor Herman Hollerith in the 1880s to assist with the 1890 United States census.*

▶ *Ada King, Countess of Lovelace, is considered to be the world's first computer programmer, writing several computer programs for Charles Babbage's Analytical Engine. King's computer programs were coded onto cards with holes punched in them.*

The advances in hardware are more obvious. A typical desktop personal computer can now store 256 megabytes (256 million bytes) of information in its RAM. One byte is a unit of information equivalent to eight binary digits—a combination of eight zeros and ones of binary code. One byte is used to represent one letter of the alphabet, a punctuation mark, or a single digit. Therefore, 256 megabytes could store five hundred novels or all the words in the *Encyclopædia Britannica*. Just 50 years ago, the Electronic Numerical Integrator and Calculator (ENIAC)—the first true general-purpose electronic computer—could store about 200 bytes.

A modern personal computer typically works at 2.8 billion cycles per second, that is, 2.8 billion steps per second. Therefore, it can do one simple mathematical task, such as adding two numbers, at each step. So it can do 2.8 billion additions per second. In 1950, ENIAC worked at 5,000 steps per second. So a modern personal computer is thus half a million times faster than ENIAC and can work with a million times as much information.

When ENIAC first began operation, it did not work using software. ENIAC did not store programs internally, and the information and instructions were written out for human use. Technicians pushed electrical leads into holes in "plugboards" to make connections that represented the information and instructions the computer needed for a particular problem. The first "stored-program" computer was an experimental machine called The Baby, which was developed at the University of Manchester, England. In June 1948, it ran what is regarded as the first modern computer program, which was written by English electrical engineer Tom Kilburn (1921–2001). Kilburn's program contained 17 instructions to enable The Baby to solve a math problem. This early computer completed the task after a few million steps in 52

DID YOU KNOW?

Ada King, Countess of Lovelace, foresaw possibilities for the Analytical Engine that were far ahead of her time. She predicted that "the Engine might compose elaborate and scientific pieces of music of any degree of complexity or extent." Because it used punched cards, similar to those used to operate Jacquard looms, she also stated that the Analytical Engine "weaves algebraical patterns just as the Jacquard loom weaves flowers and leaves," hinting that it might also be able to create attractive designs. However, King did not believe that the Analytical Engine could ever do any original thinking. In modern terminology, she did not think that genuine artificial intelligence (AI) could ever be achieved.

minutes. The Baby was later developed into the Ferranti Mark I—the first commercially available stored-program computer.

Modern software is huge and vastly complex. The software needed to control a space shuttle launch or a national telephone network, for example, consists of hundreds or thousands of linked programs and many millions of instructions.

Speeding up human-machine communication

In 1950, computer programs were developed on paper, and then the instructions were typed on a keyboard as punched patterns of holes in paper tape or in cards. Originally, the programs were in the form of symbols called machine code, which the computer could "recognize" directly. Soon after, it became possible to write programs in "assembly language," which consisted of abbreviations that were easier for the programmer to remember. These programs then had to be translated into machine code by part of the computer.

DID YOU KNOW?

The word *bug* has been used to describe faults in electrical equipment since the late nineteenth century. In September 1945, however, computer operators working on the Mark II Aiken Relay Calculator at Harvard University wrote in their log: "First actual case of bug being found." They taped the bug onto the page. It was a moth that had flown into a relay—a mechanical switch that opens and closes rapidly. The moth had been killed and had stopped the machine from working. The team boasted that they had "debugged" the machine. Ever since, computer experts have talked of "debugging" programs.

▼ *Children attend a computer science class at a school in Moscow, Russia. Computer science is now an integral part of most school curricula.*

In the late 1950s, the first programming languages were devised. Instructions in Formula Translation (FORTRAN) resembled mathematics. Instructions written in Common Business-Oriented Language (COBOL) were intended to be easily understood by business users and were written in English.

Things were made easier when users could type their programs in and see them displayed on computer monitors. Languages such as Beginner's All-Purpose Symbolic Instruction Code (BASIC) were developed to detect mistakes in individual instructions as they were written. This speeded up software development enormously, but it was still possible for a program consisting of correctly written instructions to be flawed.

Software engineering

By the mid-1970s, computers were widely used in business and universities. At first, the programs for them were written specifically for their users, either by their own departments or by the companies that made the computers. However, different programs would use standard subprograms, which could be used again in other programs. For example, doing a particular sort of calculation or displaying words and images on a screen would be jobs that could be done in the same way by many different programs. Programs and subprograms would be kept in "libraries" to be reused in new programs and on different computers.

People started to talk about "software" rather than programs because a computer would typically use many different programs, and these programs would be making use of large numbers of subprograms. Software began to be written by specialized companies. With the arrival of personal computers in the 1980s, both in the home and in business, software was sold for use across a wide range of machines. Today, many large corporations concentrate on developing software. The most famous of these is Microsoft Corporation, which made its founder, William Gates (1955–), the richest person in the world.

The millions of instructions involved in modern software need thousands of hours of development work by highly skilled specialists called software engineers. Although the individual instructions may be easy to understand, getting a sequence of

▲ *Transaction-processing software determines whether or not it is possible to withdraw cash from an automated teller machine (ATM). For example, the ATM will ask a customer for a personal identification number (PIN) to check his or her identity.*

DID YOU KNOW?

In September 1999, the multimillion-dollar *Climate Orbiter* probe burned up in the atmosphere of Mars as it tried to enter orbit around the planet. The software that controlled the probe from Earth used traditional British measurements instead of metric ones. As a result, *Climate Orbiter* was hundreds of miles away from its calculated position when it reached Mars. Less than three months later, the *Polar Lander* probe crashed on Mars. A software error caused its landing rockets to shut down too soon.

instructions to work properly, without contradicting each other or causing unintended things to happen, is a difficult and time-consuming task. A mistake in a computer program that leads either to the program failing to run, or else running but giving the wrong result (for example, giving the wrong result to a mathematical calculation), is called a "bug." First, the subprograms are tested separately before being combined into the larger programs. No matter how thoroughly the subprograms are tested, however, further testing of the entire program will be needed. After the first version of a computer program has been written, a lot of time is taken to "debug" it, testing the program and removing any errors.

See also: COMPUTER • COMPUTER GRAPHICS • DIGITAL AUDIO SOFTWARE • VIDEOPHONE • VIRTUAL REALITY

Soil

Soil is the thin layer of loose material that covers most of Earth's surface. It stores heat, food, and water for plants and is therefore one of Earth's most important natural resources. Plants would not grow without soil, and the animals that rely on plants for food would also perish.

Some soils consist of loose material that has been worn away in one place and then picked up and deposited in a new place by natural forces. Others consist of rotted pieces of the underlying rock. This process, called weathering, goes on all the time, so the composition of soils is constantly changing.

Most soils contain varying amounts of organic (once living) material, including the remains of dead plants and animals and animal droppings. All this material breaks down to form a sticky substance called humus. Humus helps bind the soil and keep it damp. It also supplies plants with nutrients. Soils rich in humus are usually very dark.

Soils appear to be solid, but about 40 percent by volume consists of air- and water-filled spaces between the grains. Soils are therefore porous (water can pass through) unless they are frozen.

The soil is home to many different organisms— tens of millions per cubic yard (meter). These range from microscopic creatures such as bacteria and fungi to earthworms and burrowing animals. Bacteria and fungi break down dead organisms to form humus, while the burrowing action of earthworms and other animals aerates the soil.

Soil horizons

Although some soils in hot countries can be up to 40 feet (12 meters) deep, most are only a few feet deep. A slice through the soil, called a soil profile,

▶ *Scientists take soil core samples from a field near Fort Collins, Colorado. The core samples will yield information on the soil horizons and their physical and chemical properties.*

▶ *Well-developed soils, such as this one from a wet, temperate (mild) region, have three horizons. Horizon A contains organic material. Horizon B consists of weathered bedrock and material leached (washed) out of horizon A. Horizon C merges into the parent rock.*

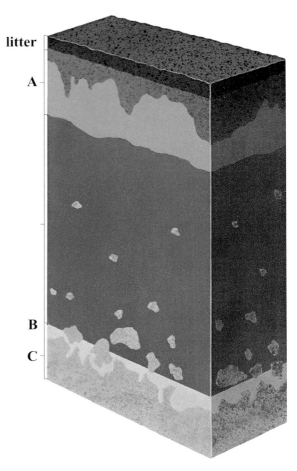

litter
A
B
C

shows that most soils contain three layers, which are called the A, B, and C horizons. The thicknesses of these horizons vary from soil to soil.

The top, or A, horizon contains most of the organic material and most of the living organisms in the soil. In wet regions, however, rain water dissolves organic nutrients from the A horizon in a process called leaching. Depleted of its nutrients, the A horizon will not support such a diverse array of living creatures.

The rain water that seeps through the A horizon often leaves some of these nutrients in the middle (B) horizon. When the A horizon is leached and the B horizon is richer in plant nutrients, farmers must plow deeply to mix the two layers.

The lowest layer of the soil, called the C horizon, is also known as the subsoil. This part contains bedrock that has begun to decay, and it merges into the solid rock below.

NATURAL SOIL

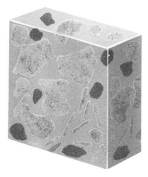

SOIL IN PARTS

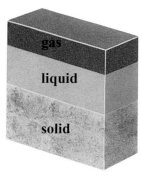

gas
liquid
solid

◀ *Soils consist of three types of materials: solid particles, liquid, and gas. The solid particles are mostly weathered (broken up) fragments of rock, with the finest particles near the surface. The topsoil of most soils also contains organic material, called humus, which consists of the decayed remains of dead plants and animals. The liquid in the soil is water, and the gas is air. Engineers want to know how the soils on building sites will behave, and they analyze soils to figure out the proportions of solids, liquid, and gas in them.*

Soil fertility

Fertile soils contain the chemical elements that support life. Some of these elements are needed in fairly large amounts. They include calcium, carbon, hydrogen, iron, magnesium, nitrogen, oxygen, phosphorus, sodium, and sulfur. Other elements are needed only in tiny amounts. They include boron, copper, iodine, manganese, and zinc. Some elements come from the air as gases, some come from water in the soil, some come from humus, and others come from the weathered bedrock.

Farming a piece of land without using fertilizers soon depletes the soil of nutrients. Soil fertility is also reduced by leaching—most wet regions have less fertile and more acidic soils than drier regions.

Soil and climate

Climate plays a big part in the formation of different soils. It affects the rate at which rocks are weathered, the amount of water in the soil, and the temperatures at which rapid or slow chemical changes are encouraged. Climate also affects soil

plants take advantage of the situation and grow quickly, but there are no trees. Tundra soils are often badly drained. The remains of dead plants form a brown, peaty surface. Lower down, the soil is normally gray and heavily leached.

South of the tundra in the Northern Hemisphere is a vast belt of coniferous forest, containing trees that produce cones, such as firs and pines. This merges farther south into a mixed coniferous and broadleaf forest. The most common type of soil there is podsol. (*Podsol* is a Russian word meaning "ash.") Cold winters do not suit the tiny animals that feed on dead plants, and so the half-decayed remains of plants pile up on the surface. Gradually, the organic matter becomes acidic as it ferments on the surface. Acid water then leaches the soil, which is gray in color. Similar soils occur in regions that once supported broadleaf forests. They are grayish-brown because iron and humus are present. They are less acidic and more fertile than true podsols.

Heavily leached soils in hot regions are called latosols or tropical red earths. They were once called laterites, but this term is now used for a special kind of latosol, which is mined for bauxite (aluminum oxide; Al_2O_3). High temperatures and

▲ *This picture shows severe soil erosion in a wheat field near Washington State University.*

through its influence on plants. Just as climate controls which plants will grow in a given region, it also greatly affects the soil in which the plants grow.

Soils in humid lands

Regions with plenty of rainfall have leached and infertile soil. Most plants find it difficult to grow in this type of soil, though it often supports large forests, since woody plants can store plant nutrients.

Stretching across northern Canada, Alaska, and Siberia is a region called the tundra. There, the subsoil is often frozen throughout the year. It is called permafrost, and it keeps water from draining down through the soil horizons. During the short summer, the top layers of the soil thaw. Various

▶ *Heathland soil, or podsol, is often acidic. Organic material decomposes very slowly in podsol.*

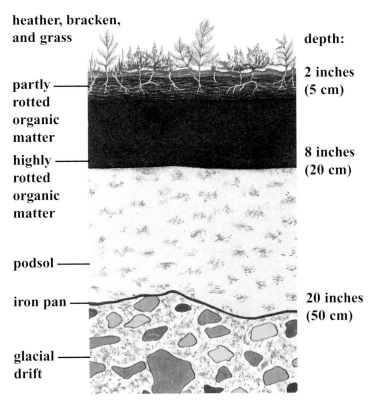

heather, bracken, and grass

partly rotted organic matter

highly rotted organic matter

podsol

iron pan

glacial drift

depth:

2 inches (5 cm)

8 inches (20 cm)

20 inches (50 cm)

heavy rain enable chemical weathering to occur deep down in the soil. Latosols are therefore deep soils. They are rich in iron and aluminum and are red or yellow.

Soils in dry lands

Soils in places with moderate or little rainfall are not heavily leached. Grass is the most natural plant in these regions. The grass and other plants form plenty of humus. Also, instead of chemicals being washed out of the A horizon, they are often brought up by rising water. Water rises upward when there is intense evaporation on the surface. The water often brings up lime from the C horizon and deposits it in the A horizon.

The soils of grasslands are called chernozems, which is a Russian word meaning "black earth." The soil is colored by humus, which is in great supply—often to depths of 3 to 4 feet (1 to 1.2 meters). Chernozems make very fertile farmland, especially for grains. Prairie soils are of this type.

Some semiarid (partially dry) regions have unleached, chestnut-brown soils. Soils in deserts are low in humus. They are usually light red, brown, or yellow.

Other soils

A classification of soils based only on climate is complicated by many other factors. For example, mountains have changing climates according to the altitude. In addition, soils do not develop as well on sloping land as they do on flat land.

Some soils are formed from material that has been dumped there by natural processes. Some of the world's most fertile soils are made of alluvium. Alluvium is a fine substance carried by fast-flowing rivers. Some of the alluvium is spread over river valleys or dropped in deltas. In warm, humid (damp) countries, these alluvial plains make rich farmland. They are among the world's most densely populated places.

Soils can be classified (grouped) in many other ways. According to their texture, for example, sandy soils are coarse-grained, silt is medium-grained, and clay soils are very fine-grained.

▲ *These huge sculptures in Cambodia have been sculpted out of latosol, which is a hard soil that forms in warm, wet regions. Latosol is heavily leached and is colored red by the presence of iron oxides.*

See also: ACID AND ALKALI • ELEMENT, CHEMICAL • EROSION • FERTILIZER • WEATHERING • WEATHER SYSTEM

Solar energy

All living things need energy from the Sun, called solar energy, to stay alive. Since energy supplies from fossil fuels, such as gas and oil, will eventually run out, scientists have been looking at different ways of using solar energy, so it can be even more useful.

The Sun radiates a huge amount of energy every day—roughly 380 million million million megawatts, which is equivalent to the total amount of energy everyone on Earth would use in 27 years. About 4 million tons (3.6 million tonnes) of the Sun's mass burns up in nuclear reactions every second. Most of this energy produced inside the Sun flows out into space, and only a tiny fraction reaches Earth's protective atmosphere. Again, only a tiny fraction of this can penetrate the atmosphere to warm the surface of the planet.

The solar energy that reaches Earth's surface heats up the land and water and makes the water in the rivers and oceans evaporate. Less than 2 percent is converted into wind and wave energy and chemical energy in plants. Windmills and other conservation methods are used to harness some of this energy. Given that all the solar energy that reaches Earth in two weeks is equivalent to the energy in all the fossil fuels locked away inside Earth's crust, very little is exploited at the moment. The problem is that huge collectors are needed to capture enough solar energy to be useful. Until the price of fossil fuels becomes too high, it will be too expensive to use solar energy on a large scale.

Heating water using the Sun

When solar energy strikes an object that absorbs light, the temperature of the object will increase. The energy in the sunlight has changed into low-temperature heat. This type of low-temperature solar-energy absorber is already used to supply hot

▲ *This close-up shows the many thousands of small mirrors that make up the parabolic reflector at the Odeillo Font-Romeu solar power station in the eastern Pyrenees, France.*

water to several million homes around the world, in countries such as Australia, Israel, and Japan. The absorbers consist of flat plates placed in panels and fixed onto the roof of a house. The panels are made to point south in the Northern Hemisphere and north in the Southern Hemisphere, and they are tilted, so they collect as much direct sunshine as possible. Cold water is pumped through the panels and warms up in the sunshine. The water pump is controlled automatically, so water flows only when the solar panel is several degrees hotter than the

◀ *Solar panels using silicon solar cells provide electricity for a house in Nicasio, California.*

water storage tank. Often, a booster heater is added to the tank, so extra heat is available if there is a long, cloudy spell.

These solar panels are about 45 to 65 percent efficient, that is, 45 to 65 percent of the sunlight falling on them is converted into useful heat.

Different ways of collecting sunlight

The problem with solar panels is that the Sun does not always shine when it is most needed, especially in more northerly latitudes. However, a well-designed solar collector could still save around 50 percent of the cost of providing hot water, even in colder climates. Instead of using panels to heat the water directly, the solar energy can be used to produce warm water, which can then be pumped and raised to a higher temperature.

Although solar power has been used in hot-water systems, scientists have not yet developed an efficient way of heating rooms. One idea is to build houses with huge cavity walls using solar energy. These are double walls with a small space between them. The space could be filled with a heat-storage material. The building would also be well insulated, so it would not need much additional heat.

Another form of solar energy is to use a photo-chemical reaction, which is a chemical reaction involving light. The reaction has to be reversible. First, solar energy is used to kick-start the reaction to make a different chemical with a lot of energy. Because the reaction is reversible, the new chemical changes back to the starter material, releasing energy in the process. So, even though solar energy comes in bursts during the day, the stored heat energy can be released day and night. The problems with this system are that the starter materials are rare and expensive to produce, and they must be used in large quantities.

Fluorescent collectors

Scientists are now using fluorescent collectors, which glow when exposed to light, to concentrate sunlight before it is directed onto photoelectric cells (cells that make electricity using energy from sunlight). The sunlight is collected over a large area and then channeled to concentrate it onto a much smaller area of cells.

This system is called a luminescent greenhouse collector. It consists of a framework of two sheets or plates of glass or plastic with a layer of fluorescent dye between. The dye soaks up the sunlight and then radiates the light at a different wavelength. The light emitted by the dye gets trapped between the plates and bounces from side to side until it reaches the edges of the plates. The sunlight is concentrated and channeled toward the photoelectric cells. The advantage of this device is that the cells do not need to be directed toward the Sun because they gather sunlight from all directions. This method is about 32 percent efficient and might be produced economically. However, suitable dyes and the right type of plastic sheet are still in development.

Using mirrors

Mirrors can also be used to concentrate sunlight before it is converted into electricity. The mirror must be in a curved shape called a parabola. Parabolic mirrors reflect all the light that falls onto them onto a single point called the focus. If a medium-sized mirror is pointed directly at the Sun, it can produce temperatures of up to 1020°F (550°C). The heat focused by the mirror can then be gathered by a heat-absorber pipe system. A liquid is pumped through the pipe, carrying the heat to where it can be used.

This idea can be carried one stage further by replacing one huge, curved mirror with hundreds, or even thousands, of small, flat mirrors. These mirrors are all pointed so that they follow the Sun. This system is called a central receiver collector, and such a system is being used at the Sandia Laboratories in New Mexico. A similar installation has been built at Odeillo in the French Pyrenees. The solar tower at the Sandia Laboratories has 1,775 mirrors. Their focus is at a steam-raising boiler atop a 200-foot (62-meter) tower. The tower does not yet generate electricity but is used to test a series of different heliostats—the mirrors that bounce the light onto the boiler. This system is a test for an advanced solar power 100-megawatt electric generating station.

The idea is that 20,000 heliostats would follow the Sun and focus the sunlight onto a liquid sodium-filled receiver. Liquid sodium is much better at absorbing heat than water, so much less sodium is needed to do the job. The sodium-carrying heat system could channel the heat from the tower to a nearby boiler room. At the boiler room, the liquid sodium would be used to heat water, raise steam, and drive turbines.

The output from a solar power station is at the mercy of the weather. However, the idea is to have a network of solar power plants spread over a wide

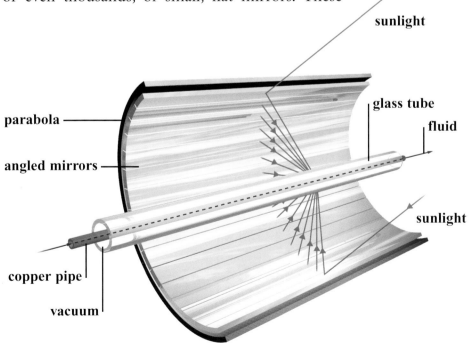

sunlight

glass tube

fluid

sunlight

parabola

angled mirrors

copper pipe

vacuum

◀ *This illustration shows a parabolic trough-type solar collector. Sunlight reaching the collector is reflected by mirrors onto the vacuum-filled glass tube. The copper pipe within the tube absorbs the heat radiation that crosses the vacuum. Like most metals, copper will lose a lot of heat by conduction but very little by radiation. Therefore, copper conducts heat to the fluid moving through the pipe but does not radiate much heat back across the vacuum.*

▲ *Receiver stations use thousands of tracking mirrors, called heliostats, to concentrate sunlight onto a receiver atop a tower. The receiver uses fluid to transfer heat to a conventional generator, such as a steam-turbine system, which generates electricity.*

geographical area and joined in a similar way to some national electricity grids. The total energy flow would then be reliable, even if there were quite strong differences in local output.

Where is solar power used now?
Several million homes already use solar power, but it is also useful for small-scale energy needs in some developing countries and for some rural uses. For example, it can be used to produce alcohol from the fermentation of plant material. Solar power removes the need for expensive distillation using coal or oil.

A safe, economic solar-powered automobile has yet to be developed, but a race across Australia in 1987 brought it much closer to reality. Energy-collecting photovoltaic cells were mounted on 25 racing cars from seven countries, with backup solar-charged batteries to help when the Sun was not shining and for climbing hills. The winner of the race was a vehicle called *GM Sunraycer*. Its solar panel carried ultraefficient solar cells of the type used on communications satellites. *GM Sunraycer* completed the 1,880-mile (3,030-kilometer) race from Darwin to Adelaide in 5½ days at an average speed of 42 miles (68 kilometers) per hour.

Solar homes of the future
All well-insulated buildings designed to work at comfortable temperatures are really in part solar heated, although they are not usually thought of as

solar buildings. In Wallasey, England, a school has been built that is heated almost entirely by solar energy but also by the lighting used in the building and the students' own body heat. It has been built with a south-facing wall of glass combined with three other walls that have been well insulated. Because the building is so large, it heats up and cools down very slowly, preventing any sudden changes in temperature. The problem still to be solved, however, is how to get enough fresh air into the building without losing too much heat.

Solar water heaters can also be used to provide heat for rooms, but then large areas of collectors are needed to provide the hot water required, and this then has to be stored in large tanks. In California, scientists have been testing a system in which a shallow reservoir is built atop a house. When the building has to be heated in winter, the reservoir is covered with a black sheet that absorbs solar energy and warms the water. This can be used to heat the house at night. During the summer, the reservoir is covered with a white sheet that reflects the Sun's energy and keeps the water cool. This can then be used to cool the house. The cost of installing these systems is high, but over many years this cost is balanced by the saving in fuel costs.

▼ **GM Sunraycer** *was designed and built by General Motors, Hughes Aircraft, and AeroVironment. In 1987, this solar-powered vehicle won the World Solar Challenge Race from Darwin to Adelaide in Australia, finishing the race in 5½ days.*

Solar ponds

A solar pond is a body of water in which the top of the pond can be frozen, and the water near the bottom can be hot. Solar ponds exist naturally in Israel, Romania, the United States, and in the Antarctic. Scientists are now trying to construct artificial solar ponds as a cheap, pollution-free source of energy.

In most natural ponds and lakes, the Sun's energy is used by the plant life, and any leftover energy that heats the bottom of the pond slowly rises to the top to be replaced by colder, heavier water. The warm water then loses its heat to the air.

In some natural ponds, the heat can be stored in the bottom layers because the water contains a high concentration of salts. Water that contains as much dissolved salt as it can is much heavier than freshwater. Sometimes a salt-laden layer of water can settle at the bottom of a pond with less salty water above. As the Sun shines on the pond, the bottom layers warm up and will store the heat as long as there is a big enough difference in salt concentration between the lower and upper layers. The more the Sun shines, the higher the temperature increases at the bottom of the pond. Eventually, the temperature of the bottom reaches a peak as high as 212°F (100°C), which is the boiling point of water.

Many small towns in the United States are of a size and have a climate that would make them able to use solar ponds effectively. A town with a

▲ *Attached to the robotic arm of the Space Shuttle Discovery, the Hubble Space Telescope is raised into the sunlight during the second servicing mission in February 1997. The golden "wings" of solar electric cells are used to power the telescope.*

population of 30,000 and with fairly large areas of unproductive land uses about three-quarters of its fuel for low-temperature water supplies and for heating rooms. A dozen or so solar ponds would take up an area of about 400 acres (160 hectares), about 2 percent of the town's land, and could supply about 98 percent of the town's low-heat needs using water between 130°F and 160°F (55°C and 75°C). The solar pond heat can be converted simply to electricity using a freon generator. Such ponds could free small towns from their dependence on expensive imported fossil fuels.

Power from space

Above the clouds of Earth's atmosphere, solar cells can receive 70 percent more sunlight. A solar power satellite (SPS) could convert the solar power into electrical power, change that into microwave radiation at 2450 megahertz, and send it to Earth in a narrow beam. Some people fear that the microwave radiation would be hazardous, but studies have shown that a low-power beam would be both workable and safe.

A typical SPS design would have two large collector panels. The two panels would be separated by a gap to support a microwave antenna. The entire assembly would be 7½ miles (12 kilometers) long and 2½ miles (4.3 kilometers) wide. Because it is so large, the SPS would have to be built entirely in space. A satellite that large would weigh about 20,000 tons (18,150 tonnes) and would need a workforce of about five hundred people to build it. It could be built in a low orbit around Earth, where it could easily be reached by a system such as the National Aeronautics and Space Administration (NASA) space shuttle. It would have to be towed up into a higher orbit for operation, however, which would require an enormous amount of fuel. Even then, the forces from the large rockets needed to tow it might make it break up.

It would therefore be necessary to build the SPS in the desired Earth orbit. Several hundred flights by a vehicle capable of carrying heavy loads would be needed to complete one SPS. At the moment, the NASA shuttle can lift a maximum of 30 tons to low-Earth orbit and can make about 40 flights a year. So some other form of space transportation must be developed before any of these SPSs can be built.

Several hundred SPSs would be needed if space-based energy were to be used on a global scale. The costs and the technical problems are huge. Sending up hundreds of missions would also cause a pollution problem, and the microwave beam might adversely affect the ionosphere (part of Earth's atmosphere). Perhaps far into the future, however, in another century, the world might use solar energy in this way.

See also: ALTERNATIVE FUEL VEHICLE • ENERGY • MICROWAVE RADIATION • PHOTOELECTRIC CELL • SATELLITE • SPACE SHUTTLE • SUN

Solar system

The solar system includes the Sun and the bodies that orbit it—the planets, their moons, comets, asteroids, and meteors. The stars that appear in the night sky may be the centers of their own solar systems.

The solar system has nine planets and a great many smaller bodies moving around a single star, called the Sun. The solar system is divided into two halves, which gives astronomers an important clue to how it formed. The first four planets away from the Sun—Mercury, Venus, Earth, and Mars—are solid planets consisting of rock and metal. They are called the terrestrial planets because their structures are similar to Earth's.

Beyond Mars lies a ring of large rocks called the asteroid belt. This is the dividing line of the solar system. In the outer reaches of the solar system are four giant planets—Jupiter, Saturn, Uranus, and Neptune. They are all much larger than the terrestrial planets. They have small rocky cores, but most of the mass of these planets consists of thick gases and ices. Jupiter and Saturn are known as gas giants, while Uranus and Neptune are the ice giants.

The most distant planet is tiny Pluto—a frozen ball of ice and rock that weaves across the orbit of Neptune at the outer edge of the solar system. Many astronomers think that Pluto is not a true planet at all, but possibly an escaped moon of Neptune or a large comet.

The fact that the planets split into two distinct groups is one clue to the way in which the solar system formed. Another clue is that 99 percent of the material in the solar system is concentrated in the Sun. In terms of mass, the planets are not important.

However, the planets and their moons account for 99 percent of the solar system's motion, as they rotate about their axes and move in their orbits.

Origin of the solar system

According to radioactive dating of meteorites and moon samples, the Sun and planets formed 4.5 billion years ago. The planets grew out of the material left over from the formation of the Sun.

Even now, astronomers can see stars forming in space. They are born inside nebulas—giant clouds of gas, dust, and ice. A nebula gradually shrinks under the inward pull of its own gravity. The nebula then breaks up into smaller, denser clumps, which are the first stages of new solar systems.

At the center of the clump, the density of the gas increases rapidly as the clump shrinks. As the gases at the center are pressed together more tightly, they heat up. Eventually, the temperature and pressure at the center of the clump become so extreme that nuclear fusion takes place. This reaction involves two hydrogen atoms merging to make an atom of helium. This fusion releases huge amounts of heat and light. The clump of gas has now become a star.

▶ This picture of the Sun was taken by NASA's Solar and Heliospheric Observatory satellite. Two huge solar prominences are erupting from the Sun's surface. Prominences are jets of superhot gas.

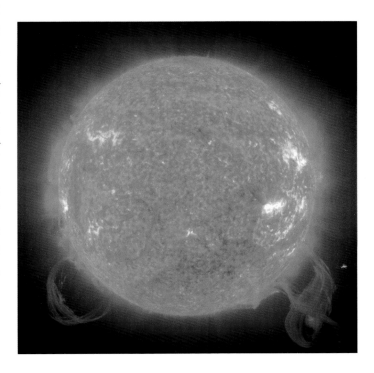

	Mercury	Venus	Earth	Mars	Jupiter	Saturn	
Distance from Sun, millions of miles (km)	36 (58)	67 (108)	93 (150)	142 (228)	486 (778)	891 (1,427)	
Period of revolution about Sun (year)	88 days	225 days	365 days	687 days	11.9 years	29.5 years	
Rotation period relative to stars	59 days (W to E)	243 days (E to W)	23 hr 56 min (W to E)	24 hr 37 min (W to E)	9 hr 55 min (W to E)	10 hr 39 min (W to E)	
Day length	176 days	120 days	24 hours	24 hr 39 min	9 hr 50 min	10 hr 14 min	
Diameter, miles (km)	3,048 (4,878)	7,563 (12,102)	7,972 (12,756)	4,245 (6,792)	89,365 (142,984)	75,355 (120,536)	
Mass (relative to Earth)	0.055	0.81	1.00	0.11	318	95	
Satellites (as of 2004)	0	0	1	2	62	37	

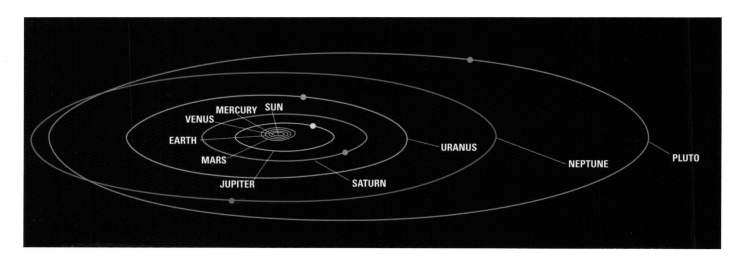

Not all the gas, dust, and ice of the shrinking cloud falls into the star at its center. As it shrinks, the cloud spins more quickly, and this spreads the contents of the cloud out into a disk shape. The planets are formed from this disk by a process known as accretion; material gradually builds up, forming larger and larger bodies.

Building the planets

In the doughnut-shaped cloud orbiting the young star, the tiny dust and ice grains often crash into each other. Sometimes they stick together, forming loose, lightweight fluffy balls. As these bodies grow, their gravitational pull also increases, and they begin to attract each other. This drives the second stage of growth, with bodies sticking together.

Many millions of bodies would make a single solid, called a planetesimal, a few miles across. Near the young Sun, the temperature would have been so high that all the ices in the planetesimals would melt and evaporate, leaving planetesimals made of rocks and metals. Farther away from the Sun, it would have been colder, so the planetesimals would be mostly ice, with only small amounts of rock.

Uranus	Neptune	Pluto
1,794 (2,871)	2,815 (4,504)	3,666 (5,900)
84 years	165 years	248 years
17 hr 14 min (E to W)	16 hr 6 min (W to E)	6 days 9 hr (E to W)
17 hr 14 min	16 hr 6 min	6 days 9 hr
31,949 (51,118)	30,955 (49,528)	1,438 (2,302)
15	17	0.002
27	13	1

◀ *This scale diagram shows the position of the planets' orbits around the Sun. The four inner planets are crowded close to the Sun, whereas the five outer planets orbit the Sun at much greater distances.*

▲ NASA's **Magellan** *probe mapped the surface of Venus in the early 1990s. Magellan used radar beams to scan and reveal the solid surface beneath the planet's thick clouds.*

In the third stage of planet formation, the ten billion or so planetesimals orbiting around the Sun came together. Planetesimals that passed near each other would be pulled together, forming larger planetesimals. The largest planetesimals would gradually have swept up nearby smaller ones. In this way, all the small planetesimals would blend into the nine planets seen today.

In the cold outer parts of the solar system, the forming planets would have pulled thick atmospheres of gas around them. In the inner part of the solar system, the rocky Earth-like planets may have had temporary atmospheres, but these would have been blown away by the heat of the Sun. According to geologists, the atmospheres of the inner planets have leaked out through volcanoes.

Sweeping up

However, there is one other problem to be solved. Astronomers believe that the shrinking gas clump needed to form the Sun would have had much more mass than is present in the solar system today. In fact, about 90 percent of the original cloud that collapsed to form the solar system has vanished. Where has it gone? It has probably been blown away by the energy of the Sun.

Astronomers studying young stars have found that strong winds of gas are blowing away from them. Such stars are known as T Tauri stars, after the first of their kind to be observed (in the constellation Taurus). T Tauri stars are surrounded by clouds of gas that seem to be scattering as a result of the energy being radiated by the young, powerful star. This is the same process that cleaned up Earth's solar system.

Solar wind

Even now, a gentle wind blows outward from the Sun. This solar wind is a stream of atomic particles that flows through the solar system. The solar wind was much more energetic in the early days of the solar system. The solar wind could have stripped

▶ *This is an artist's impression of Saturn and its moons using images taken by the Voyager 1 probe. The moon in the foreground is Dione, with Saturn rising behind. Two other moons, called Tethys and Mimas, can be seen in the distance to the right. Enceladus and Rhea can be seen by Saturn's rings to the left, and the largest moon, Titan, is shown in its distant orbit at the top.*

the atmospheres from the inner planets and scattered the gases that had not collected into planets. It could also have slowed down the speed of the Sun's rotation.

Even with the leftover gas swept out of the solar system, the cleaning-up operation was not yet complete. A number of planetesimals were too heavy for the solar wind to sweep away and continued to orbit the Sun. Some of these settled down into orbits between Mars and Jupiter and formed the asteroid belt. The gravity of Jupiter prevented them from gathering together into a tenth planet. Others were captured by the planets to form moons. Still others, which formed in the cold outer parts of the solar system, stayed in a belt beyond the known planets called the Kuiper belt. Even farther out, icy planetesimals formed a cloud around the solar system. This sphere is called the Oort cloud. Occasionally, members of the Kuiper belt or Oort cloud are pulled into the center of the solar system on very long orbits. These bodies are called comets. As it approaches the Sun, the ice on a comet's surface begins to evaporate, producing a long glowing tail that points away from the Sun.

Finally, many of the smaller objects that had failed to hit the planets the first time were gradually swept up by the planets in their final stages of accretion. For more than 700 million years, asteroid-sized bodies and smaller meteorites have slammed into the planets and have ground their surfaces to powder. The surfaces of Mercury, Mars, and the moons of the planets now show the results of this bombardment, and the process has not entirely ceased—small rocks from space often blaze their way into Earth's atmosphere.

Other solar systems?

Planets seem to be a normal by-product of the birth of stars, so astronomers are looking for other solar systems in space. However, planets are so small compared to their stars that they are difficult to spot. Many disk-shaped clouds around young stars are probably filled with planetesimals. To date, nearly 150 planets have been found through the visible wobble of the stars they revolve around.

See *also:* SPACE PROBE • STAR • SUN

Solenoid

A solenoid is a coil of wire through which an electrical current is passed to set up a magnetic field inside the coil. This magnetic force can be used to move an iron rod inside the coil to operate certain types of switches.

When a simple bar magnet is suspended from a thin thread, it will align itself in a north-south direction. The end of the magnet facing geographic north is called the north pole, and the end facing south is called the south pole.

When an electrical current is passed through a coil of wire to form a solenoid, the ends of the coil will also align in a north-south direction when the solenoid is hung horizontally. The direction of the current determines which end forms the north pole and which end forms the south pole. A iron or steel rod near the solenoid will be guided to the poles by the lines of force within the magnetic field.

▼ *This picture shows the coil inside the frame of a simple solenoid. In the solenoid, wire is coiled tightly to form a cylinder that is longer than it is wide, and this is connected to a power source (through the red leads).*

The strength of the magnetic field inside the solenoid is the same along most of its length. Toward the poles, however, the strength of the magnetic field falls to about one-half of this typical value. For the strongest magnetic force, a solenoid should therefore be infinitely long. In practice, it is possible to achieve up to 99 percent of the maximum if the solenoid is seven times as long as the diameter of its coils.

Uses of solenoids

The most important use of solenoids is as switching mechanisms that can protect one circuit in a device from a heavy current. In the solenoid, the wire coil is connected to a power source. When an electrical current flows through the coil, the magnetic field attracts a metal rod at one end of the cylinder. The rod is then drawn into the cylinder. As the rod moves into the coil, an electrical contact on the end of the rod meets with another contact for a separate circuit inside the coil. The rod activates the second circuit when the two contacts connect.

This type of switching mechanism is used in the starter motors for automobiles. Two solenoids are mounted side by side above the starter motor. A iron or steel plunger running through both has one

▶ *This illustration shows the use of solenoids in the starter motor of an internal combustion engine. One solenoid draws in the clutch, and the other holds it in position while the motor turns the engine.*

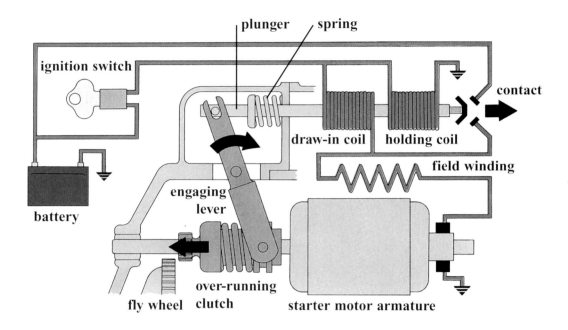

plunger   spring

ignition switch

contact

draw-in coil   holding coil

field winding

engaging lever

battery

over-running clutch

fly wheel

starter motor armature

▶ *The power-operated switch can be used to control the heating system in a home.*

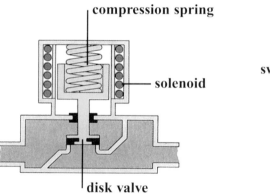

compression spring

solenoid

disk valve

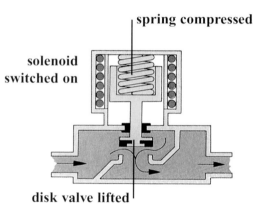

spring compressed

solenoid switched on

disk valve lifted

end attached to a lever and the other connected to a switch. Turning the ignition key sets up a low current through the "draw in" coil. This magnetizes the plunger and it moves, causing the lever to engage (interlock) the starter motor with a flywheel. At the same time, the other end of the plunger makes contact with the switch. This transfers power to the holding coil and hence to the starter motor. Once the engine is running, the ignition key is released, switching off the current.

In a simple power-operated switch, a solenoid provides the power to open and close a disk valve. Sending a current through the solenoid produces a magnetic field. This moves a rod to which the disk valve is connected and thus draws the valve away from the opening. When the current is turned off, the valve is closed again by a spring.

DID YOU KNOW?

One major problem with electromagnetic devices such as solenoids is the loss of energy through heat radiation, which is caused by eddy currents. Eddy currents are tiny transient currents that can be induced in the parts of the device that carry the magnetic field, for example, the metal rod inside the wire coil of a solenoid. As a result, these parts are often laminated to prevent eddy currents from forming.

See also: ELECTRIC MOTOR • ELECTROMAGNETISM • MAGNETISM • SWITCH

Solid

Solids are materials that do not readily change their shape. People rely on the strength and constant shape of solids to provide them with a firm, reliable world. Almost all matter can become solid if it is cooled sufficiently.

Chairs, freeways, and houses could not be made out of water. All these things need a fixed shape, and water is a liquid—it takes the shape of whatever container in which it is placed. Many of the things people depend on for support or shelter need to be solid, that is, relatively fixed in shape. The wood that makes a chair, the concrete of a freeway, and the brick, steel, and wood of a house are all examples of solid materials.

Although a solid is relatively fixed in shape, its shape can be changed if a strong enough force is applied. A strong blow can shatter glass or splinter wood. Often, a very small force is enough to alter the shape of some solids, such as rubber or putty. Even butter is a solid, although it is very soft.

Most solids melt and turn into a liquid if they are heated sufficiently. Solid and liquid are two different states of matter. Further heating will change the liquid into gas, which is another state of matter. Some substances change directly from solid

▲ *This gold ingot is typical of a metallic solid. Most metals consist of positive metal ions fixed firmly in relation to one another, with a sea of negative electrons binding the positive cores together.*

to gas when heated, without going through a liquid stage. Carbon dioxide (CO_2), which is a gas at normal conditions, is an example.

There is another state of matter. Plasma is formed at extremely high temperatures. The atoms of a plasma are broken up into positively and negatively charged particles called ions. Plasma also does not have a fixed shape.

Binding forces

Solids are fairly rigid (fixed in shape) materials because there are strong links between the atoms or molecules from which they are made. The atoms or molecules of a liquid are generally surrounded by fewer neighbors, allowing space for movement even though the attractive force between neighbors is still quite strong. A liquid therefore flows to fill the

DID YOU KNOW?

Under normal conditions, the densest elements are iridium and osmium. These metals have a density of 22,650 kilograms per cubic meter (1,415 pounds per cubic foot)—22.6 times as dense as the same volume of water. In fact, the density of iridium and osmium is so similar that scientists keep changing their minds about which metal is the most dense.

▶ *Dry ice is the solid, frozen form of carbon dioxide. The surface temperature of a block of dry ice is −108°F (−78°C). As the temperature rises, some of the carbon dioxide molecules have enough energy to break free from the forces binding them as a solid, and they are released as a vapor, without first going through a liquid stage. This effect is known as sublimation.*

bottom of any container. In the gas phase, the atoms or molecules are very far apart and only effect each other through occasional collisions. Therefore, the atoms or molecules of a gas will fill a container completely.

The atoms in a solid are joined in a network called a lattice. Often this is a regular pattern called a crystal lattice. The more perfect the pattern of atoms or molecules in the lattice, the stronger the solid. All materials have defects in the pattern, however, which means that the solid is usually weaker than it should be.

DID YOU KNOW?

The solid with the lowest density value is an artificial substance called aerogel, nicknamed "frozen smoke." Aerogel was developed by the National Aeronautics and Space Administration (NASA) for space research. It consists of a solid foam of silica (silicon dioxide; SiO_2), which is a compound found in a denser form in glass, quartz, sand, and many other materials. The density of aerogel is 3 milligrams per cubic centimeter, which is 300 times less dense than water. NASA used aerogel on the *Stardust* probe to trap interplanetary dust.

Heating a solid makes the atoms or molecules vibrate faster. The forces binding the atoms or molecules become weaker, and the solid will gradually turn into a liquid.

Conversely, cooling a gas makes the atoms or molecules move more slowly. When they are moving slowly enough, they stick together, and the gas turns into a liquid. If the liquid is cooled enough, it freezes (turns into a solid). For example, if air is cooled to very low temperatures, the oxygen in it will freeze at −369°F (−223°C). The nitrogen will freeze at −346°F (−210°C). The small amount of helium in the air will not turn into a solid until the air has been cooled to −452°F (−269°C).

The density of a solid is defined as its mass per unit volume. By international agreement, scientists express density in kilograms per cubic meter. The density of a solid does not change much under standard conditions. In Earth's interior, however, solid material is crushed so fiercely that it reaches huge densities. For example, the normal density of the metal iron is 7,900 kilograms per cubic meter (493 pounds per cubic foot). However, the iron in Earth's interior is nearly twice as dense due to the huge temperature and pressure there.

See also: ATOM AND MOLECULE • CRYSTAL • GAS • LIQUID • METAL

Sonar

The first sonar devices were used during World War I (1914–1918) to detect enemy submarines. They worked by sending sound waves under the water and waiting for the reflections that bounced off the surface of the submarine. Sonar devices are now more widely used to help control the course of ships and to find and follow schools of fish.

Most people think of sound as vibrations in the air, but water can also carry the vibrations. In fact, sound waves can travel great distances through the water and are therefore extremely useful for underwater detection. Sonar (short for "sound navigation ranging") works on a principle called echo sounding. By listening for the echoes, it is possible to build up an image of what lies beneath the surface of the water.

How sonar works

First, a short pulse of sound is transmitted from a device called a transducer, which is fixed under the ship below the surface of the water. The sound may be one that is within the range that can be heard by people, or it may be a much higher frequency.

The sound pulse travels downward and outward in all directions. If the sound strikes the seabed or a large object, such as a submarine, some of the sound will be reflected back to the ship. There, it is picked up by another transducer, and the total time taken by the pulse is recorded. Because the speed of

▼ *A sonar-imaging device has built up this picture of the USS* Monitor *using the sound waves reflected by the surface of the ship.*

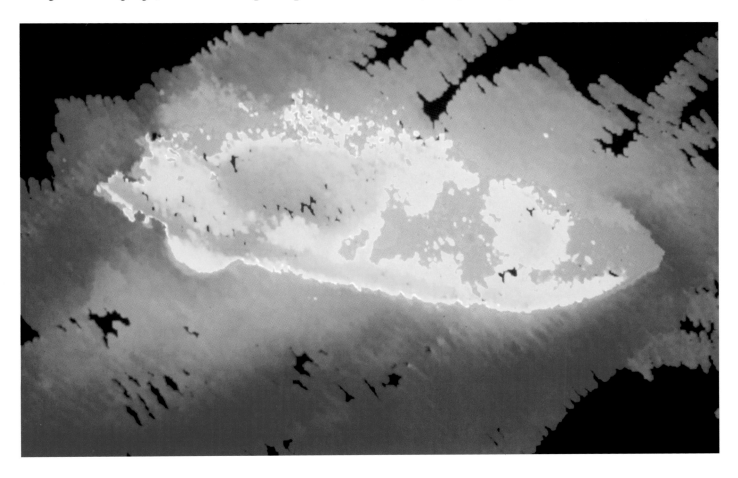

▲ *A technician aboard USS* **Nimitz** *uses sonar equipment to detect underwater submarines. Instead of being directed downward, the sound pulses are concentrated into beams that sweep the water below.*

sound in water is known to be roughly 4,800 feet (1,460 meters) per second, it is possible to figure out the distance traveled by the pulse before it was reflected back. In this way, the reflected sound is a measure of the location of the underwater object, as well as its direction and speed of travel if, like a submarine, it is moving.

Types of sonar

All modern ships carry an echo sounder to help with their navigation. This is the simplest form of sonar and is used to measure the depth of water.

Some of these devices have a rotating disk that acts as a timer. A neon tube lights up when the sound signal is returned. The timer is attached to the range measurement scale, which shows the distance traveled by the pulse. Others have a cathode ray tube (CRT) display (similar to a television screen) or a moving stylus that darkens electrically sensitive paper.

Sonar is not only used for military applications. Modern sonar devices can be used to detect and follow schools of fish, to map the seafloor, or to locate sunken ships. These devices produce detailed images of underwater objects using laser beams in a technique called holography.

Natural sonar

Some marine animals, such as porpoises, use a natural form of sonar to locate underwater objects and to communicate with each other. Marine biologists also think that certain species use sound to stun their prey or disorientate predators.

See also: NAVIGATION • TRANSDUCER

Sound

Sound travels in the form of waves through the material, or medium, within which it is moving. Sound waves can travel through air, through a liquid such as water, and even through solid materials such as metals. When sound waves reach a person's ears, the brain decodes the vibrations into sound that can be heard. The study of sound waves is called acoustics.

▲ *The vibrations of a tuning fork displace water in a glass. Tuning forks help illustrate the nature of sound as the vibration of air at a frequency that is audible to the human ear.*

When an object vibrates in the air, the air molecules next to the surface of the object are first compressed (pushed together) and then rarefied (pulled apart). These air molecules bump into neighboring air molecules, and so the next set of molecules becomes compressed and rarefied. In this way, sound travels through the air. The air molecules themselves do not move with the sound wave. The vibrations simply pass the sound along to the next set of air molecules.

When the vibrations reach the ears, they make the eardrums vibrate. These vibrations are sent through nerves to the brain, which decodes the messages into sound. People can hear sounds as low as 20 vibrations per second (20 hertz) or as high as 20,000 vibrations per second (20,000 hertz).

Sound requires a gas, liquid, or solid through which to travel; it will not pass through a vacuum (a space entirely devoid of matter). Sound travels faster through a solid medium than it does through a liquid medium. In the same way, sound travels faster through a liquid than it does through a gas. When sound passes through a piece of steel, for example, the waves travel at around 11,180 miles (18,000 kilometers) per hour. In water, however, the sound waves slow down to around 3,130 miles (5,050 kilometers) per hour. In air at normal room temperature, sound waves move at about 769 miles (1,250 kilometers) per hour.

Temperature does not have much effect on sound when it travels through a solid or a liquid, but it does when sound travels through a gas. This is because gas molecules bump into each other more quickly as temperature rises.

Different sounds

Why is the sound made by a piano different from the sound made by a trumpet? There are three properties that make one sound different from another: loudness, pitch, and quality. The loudness of a sound depends on the energy of the sound wave. Pitch refers to whether it is a high sound or a

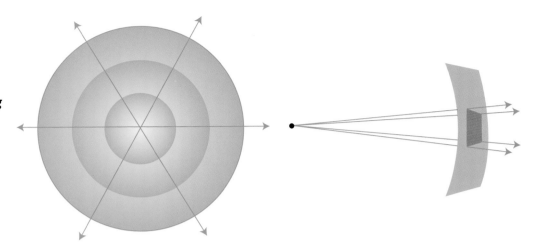

▶ *A sound wave spreads out from its source equally in all directions (left). If an observer could see the waves, he or she would see spheres of sound expanding out from the source. If the observer could see a small part of the spherical wave at a long distance from the source (right), he or she would see a series of plane waves passing by at regular intervals.*

low sound, and it depends on frequency (number of vibrations per second). The quality of a sound, or timbre, is what allows people to differentiate between two notes of the same loudness and pitch played on different musical instruments. Timbre depends on the shape of the sound wave.

HOW DO SOUND WAVES BEHAVE?

Sound waves behave like any other types of wave motion, for example, light and X-rays. Sound waves can be reflected, refracted, or diffracted, and they can interfere with each other.

Reflection

The reflection of sound is important in such buildings as auditoriums and movie theaters. These buildings are designed so that people hear sounds from different directions at various times. For example, people listening to an orchestra will hear the sound of the instruments coming from the stage, but echoes can also be heard when the sound waves bounce off the walls, ceiling, and any other objects. The time it takes for a sound to fade away is called its reverberation time.

The quality of the sound is dependent on the reverberation time. A very short reverberation time of about half a second makes an orchestra sound thin and lifeless, but too long a reverberation time can make the music sound muffled.

The reverberation time depends on the size of the room, the surface area, and the sound-absorbing characteristics of the surfaces. Some materials, such

as carpets, drapes, and upholstery, absorb sound waves well. However, hard, smooth surfaces, such as concrete, glass, and plaster, are poor absorbers of sound waves. By choosing the shapes of surfaces in an auditorium, as well as the materials from which they are to be made, the reverberation time can be adjusted before the building is constructed.

Refraction

When sound passes from one medium to another, the waves are refracted (bent away from their original path). Sound can also be refracted when there is a change in the temperature of the air through which the waves are moving. Refraction is the reason why sound is easier to hear and travels farther at night. During the day, the air near the ground is warmer than the air high above it. Sound waves are thus refracted away from Earth's surface. At night, the air near the ground is cold, and the air

▶ *This illustration shows the way in which two sound waves interfere constructively and destructively. Sound waves from the two loudspeakers (A and B) interfere constructively (crest meets crest; point C) to produce a loud sound and destructively (crest meets trough; point D) to produce little, if any, sound.*

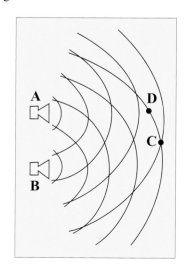

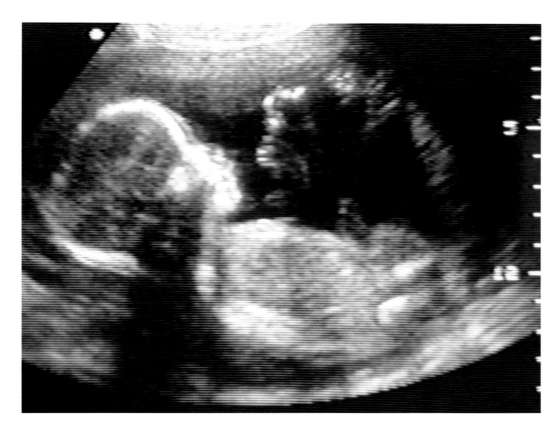

◄ *The equipment used to take this ultrasound scan transmits and then detects the echoes of the ultrasound waves as they bounce off the fetus inside the uterus. Ultrasound waves are very high frequency sound waves, that is, above 20,000 hertz.*

higher up is warm. Therefore, sounds are refracted back to Earth's surface and are louder and can be heard at longer distances.

Diffraction

Sound waves usually travel in straight lines, but they can bend around objects that are about the same size as their wavelength. The wavelengths of sound are normally between several inches and a few feet long, so they can bend around most everyday objects. Low-frequency waves are bent more easily than high-frequency waves.

Interference

Two sound waves with the same frequency will interfere with each other if they arrive at the same point after traveling different distances. The sound waves can interfere so that they reinforce each other and produce a loud sound (constructive interference), or they can interfere so that they produce a softer sound (destructive interference).

Sound waves can also interfere with each other if they have different frequencies. When the frequencies are almost the same but not identical, beats are heard. Beats like loud bursts of noise are heard over a background of quieter noise. The number of beats heard per second is called the beat frequency. Beat frequency can be used to tune one string of a musical instrument with another. The two strings are sounded together and one of them adjusted until no beats are heard.

The Doppler effect

As a police car moves toward a person standing on the street, the pitch of the sound produced by the siren increases. As the police car passes and then moves away, the pitch of the sound produced by the siren gradually falls. However, the frequency of the sound does not change. As the siren approaches, more sound waves reach the person's ears at one time than are given out in that time, so the person hears a high-pitched sound. As the vehicle passes, fewer sound waves reach the person's ears than are given out at a particular time, and the pitch of the sound drops. This phenomenon is called the Doppler effect, named for Austrian physicist Johann Christian Doppler (1803–1853), who first described the effect in 1842.

*An aircraft technician aboard USS **John F. Kennedy** wears ear guards to protect his ears from the loud roar of jet aircraft on the flight deck. It has long been realized that loud noises can cause deafness. In recent years, physicians have discovered that exposure to moderate noise can also damage the hearing.*

Ultrasound

Sound waves with frequencies of between 20 and 20,000 hertz are called audible sounds because people can hear them. Above 20,000 hertz, however, the vibrations are too fast for people to hear, although animals such as dogs and bats can detect them. Sound waves with frequencies above 20,000 hertz are said to be ultrasonic.

Ultrasound has many applications in industry and medicine. For example, the rapid vibrations of ultrasonic waves can be used for drilling. Ultrasound is also used to clean complex surfaces such as engine parts and laboratory equipment. One of the most familiar uses of ultrasound in medicine is for checking the development of the fetus in the uterus. Ultrasound images are produced as the sound waves are reflected by the tissues of the fetus.

The decibel scale

The world is full of different sounds, although most of them go unnoticed. The middle of a city park is very quiet compared to the busy streets around it. Listen carefully, however, and one will hear the noise of traffic and airplanes passing overhead.

Noise can be measured for both loudness and pitch. The common measurement is the decibel scale. On the decibel scale, a whisper registers 30 decibels, a vacuum cleaner measures 70 decibels at 10 feet (3 meters), and a jackhammer makes a noise of 100 decibels at a distance of 15 feet (4.5 meters). An increase of 10 decibels means a doubling of the volume of the sound, so 80 decibels is twice as loud as 70 decibels.

Noise pollution

Eighty decibels is considered to be the safe noise limit. It has been found that about 17 out of every 100 factory workers exposed to a constant noise level of 90 decibels during their working lives will have damaged hearing. This damage happens slowly, so the person may not notice any problems in hearing for several years.

It is often difficult or impossible to cut down the noise under certain factory conditions. For example, drop forging machines produce sudden noise levels of as much as 135 decibels, and little can be done to reduce this noise pollution. In these situations, wearing ear guards or ear plugs can protect the workers from suffering ear damage.

Amplified music is now probably the most common cause of high noise levels. A stereo set can generate 100 watts output per channel, producing noise levels of up to 115 decibels. An even more dangerous source of sound is headphones. Even with only milliwatts (thousandths of a watt) of output power, headphones can produce dangerous decibel levels of 90 to 105.

On some occasions, the level of sound produced by such equipment is so high that the ears hurt. When this happens, the sound has passed what is called the threshold of feeling. The main sensation is then one of pain, rather than sound.

See also: DOPPLER EFFECT • EAR AND HEARING • SONAR • SOUND RECORDING

Sound recording

Imagine a world where sounds, such as music and spoken words, could not be recorded and played back. Until about one hundred years ago, that was just what the world was like. People could only listen to music live. Recorded sound is now readily available on radios, stereos, televisions, and computers.

All sound is produced when something happens to make the air vibrate. For example, plucking guitar strings or blowing into a flute produces vibrations in the air, which scientists call sound waves. Blowing air through flaps of muscle in the throat, called the vocal cords, also produces sound in the form of speech.

Sound waves spread out in all directions. When they reach a person's ears, the vibrations in the air make a thin flap of skin—known as the ear drum—vibrate in the same way. Then electrical nerve pulses in the brain turn the eardrum's vibrations into the sounds people hear. Devices that record sound also detect vibrations, turning them into electrical signals.

Sound writing

For centuries, people understood that sounds produce vibrations. However, it was not understood that vibrations could also produce sounds until the end of the nineteenth century. Only then did someone realize that sound could be recorded.

The first sound-recording machine was the phonograph, which was invented by U.S. inventor Thomas Alva Edison (1847–1931). (Edison also invented many other useful devices, including the lightbulb.) The word *phonograph* means "sound writing." Edison's invention was not meant to be a music recorder. Instead, it was intended to record spoken messages.

Edison perfected his invention in 1877. The first model recorded sound on cylinders covered in tinfoil. Later, wax cylinders were used because they

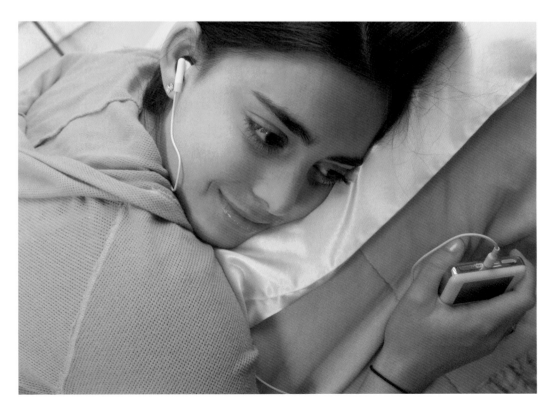

▶ Most music is now stored as digital files. These can be stored on a digital audio player. The player converts the data in the files into sounds that can be heard through headphones.

In 1887, German-born U.S. inventor Emile Berliner (1851–1929) produced the gramophone. This worked in the same way as Edison's phonograph, but sound was recorded onto flat disks, not cylinders. Gramophones, or record players as they became known, were the most popular way of playing music for the next one hundred years.

By the early twentieth century, recorded music was becoming very popular. Records needed to be copied, so they could be played on the growing number of gramophones. A metal master disk was used as a mold to make a metal stamper. This stamper was used to make thousands of identical records out of soft vinyl plastic.

Electrical recordings

Until 1925, sounds were recorded mechanically. Just the sound of a singer's voice and musical instruments were used to move the needle and cut the groove. In 1925, the first electrical recordings were made using microphones and amplifiers to boost the sound. This produced a stronger and truer reproduction of the original sound.

Microphones change sounds into electrical signals. In this form, the sound signals can be sent along wires. The telephone was the first device to make use of the microphone.

All microphones work in the same way as the diaphragm that Edison used to make his first recording. However, there are several designs of microphone depending on their application. Some microphones need to be inexpensive, and some need to reproduce sound exactly, while others need to be sensitive to quiet sounds.

Ribbon microphones are high-quality microphones used in recording and broadcasting studios. They contain a thin metal ribbon. This is supported between the poles of a permanent magnet. The ribbon acts as the diaphragm of the microphone and vibrates when struck by sound waves.

were damaged less easily and lasted longer. The very first sound recording was of Edison himself reciting the nursery rhyme *Mary Had a Little Lamb*.

Edison recorded sound onto a cylinder by speaking into a tube. The tube was attached to a metal disk, or diaphragm, which had a sharp needle sticking out the other side. The needle was placed carefully onto the cylinder. During recording, the cylinder was turned using a handle, so the needle made a groove on the cylinder's surface.

The sound waves from Edison's voice caused the diaphragm to vibrate, which in turn made the needle vibrate. The vibrating needle moved up and down as it cut the groove. A loud sound made a deep groove, while a softer sound cut a shallower groove. Therefore, the cylinder contained a tracing of the vibrations produced by the voice.

In reverse, the groove vibrated the needle, which vibrated the diaphragm. The diaphragm then produced vibrations in the air, and these vibrations were heard as Edison's voice.

When a current-carrying wire moves between two magnets, a voltage is produced. Voltage is a measure of the force that pushes electrons along wires or other conductors. This is the principle of electromagnetic induction. In the ribbon microphone, the metal ribbon is the conductor, and the voltage acting on it (and the current running through it) varies according to how much it vibrates. In other words, the varying voltage is a record of the sound wave.

Playback

Although it is a faithful copy of the original sound, the signal from a ribbon microphone is very weak, so it has to be amplified (strengthened). This makes an electrical signal that is strong enough to power a loudspeaker or to be stored in different ways.

▼ *Musicians record some music using microphones. Microphones convert sound waves into electrical signals. They detect the motion of the air and turn that movement into electricity.*

A loudspeaker works in the opposite way to a microphone. The electrical signal is supplied to an electromagnet made from a coil of wire. This is a magnet that only works when it has an electrical current running through it.

A large current makes the electromagnet very powerful—producing a large magnetic field that pushes on metal objects. A smaller current makes the magnet less strong. A varying current, similar to the one produced by a recorded sound signal, makes the electromagnet vary in strength.

The magnet in the loudspeaker pushes on a large diaphragm. When the electrical signal flows through the magnet, the magnet pushes on the diaphragm with different strengths. This makes the diaphragm wobble backward and forward. As it wobbles, the diaphragm produces vibrations in the air, which make up sound. When the diaphragm is pushed forward a long way, it produces a loud sound. When it is just moved slightly, the loudspeaker produces a quiet sound.

◄ *A disc jockey plays music with a modern record table, called a turntable. The turntable's needle reads the sound recorded on the record and converts it into an electrical signal. This signal is then converted into sound by loudspeakers.*

a 12-inch (30.5 centimeter) long-playing (LP) record is about 3 miles (4.8 kilometers) long. Although LPs and other records are rarely played on home stereos anymore, some musicians and disc jockeys (DJs) still use them to play music to audiences because they believe the sound quality is better than more modern alternatives, such as compact discs (CDs).

Before the 1950s, master disks were cut from live performances. As the musicians played into the microphones, the groove was cut into the master. In the 1950s, however, tape recordings were invented. This involved using the signal from the microphone to produce patterns on the magnetic surface of a thin, flexible tape. The pattern could be read to replay the sound.

Tape allowed sounds to be recorded and then replayed to produce the master disk. This changed the way music was made because tape recordings allowed musicians to merge several versions of a song together into one finished project.

At first, tape recorders were used only in recording studios because they were too large and complicated to use at home. In 1963, the tape cassette was invented. This is a small plastic box that contains the tape on a reel and which fits into a player easily.

Sound storage

The amplified electrical signal picked up by the microphone can also be used to produce a recording of sound. Until the 1980s, vinyl disks were the most popular way of storing music. Just like in the early days of the gramophone, each disk was pressed from a metal master. However, the master disk was produced using the electric signal, not by the sounds themselves.

The master disk was cut using a lathe—a machine with a turntable and a needle mounted on a movable arm. The needle was attached to a coiled electromagnet, similar to the ones used in loudspeakers. When the electrical signal arrived from the microphone, it made the needle wobble up and down. In the same way as Edison's first phonograph, this produced a single groove in the master disk that went up and down. The groove in

Digital recording

Most sound recordings are now stored as computer files. The files comprise long lists of numbers, or digits, so the files are often called digital recordings. Nondigital recordings are called analog. Digital recordings are produced from the microphone's signal using an analog-to-digital converter.

See also: DIGITAL AUDIO SOFTWARE •
EAR AND HEARING • LASER DISC • MAGNETIC
STORAGE • SPEECH • SOUND

Space laboratory

Laboratories orbiting high above Earth's atmosphere can use the special conditions in space to perform experiments and record observations that could not easily be done in a laboratory on the ground. They can also be used to study the Sun, stars, and other celestial bodies much more accurately than was previously possible.

▲ *The International Space Station is the largest spacecraft ever built. When the space station is completed, it will be as large as two football fields.*

Every year, hundreds of uncrewed satellites are launched into orbit around Earth. The satellites perform many tasks, including beaming television pictures and telephone calls around the world, collecting information about weather patterns, and taking detailed pictures of Earth's surface. Other satellites perform scientific experiments and make observations of the Sun, stars, or different parts of Earth. Although these satellites can work well, they generally cannot be used for any other purposes once they are in orbit.

Scientific satellites cannot be made to carry out a new experiment when the original one is completed. Space laboratories can be used to do a much wider range of tasks because they have a crew of astronauts, who can perform different experiments at once. New crews arriving from Earth can also bring the equipment they need with them.

Working in space

Space laboratories are used to investigate the effects of weightlessness on people and other living things. Because they are outside Earth's atmosphere, space laboratories also have a very clear view of objects in space, and they are often used as observatories.

Most space laboratories are located inside space stations—large satellites that have room for a crew. Other space laboratories are carried into orbit by space shuttles. They stay in space for a short while and then return to Earth along with the shuttle.

The first space laboratories

In the early years of space exploration in the 1960s, astronauts often only spent a few hours or days in space. There were plans to make longer flights, but no one knew what effects extended periods in space would have on a person's health.

By the 1970s, the longest time an astronaut had spent in orbit was 17 days. The spacecraft used in those days, such as the Apollo spacecraft used by U.S. astronauts to fly to the Moon, had no room for the crew and all the equipment needed for prolonged space experiments.

In 1971, the former Soviet Union launched the first space station, called *Salyut 1*, which contained a large working compartment where experiments could be carried out. Three Soviet cosmonauts arrived aboard a Soyuz spacecraft and lived and worked on *Salyut 1* for 22 days. However, the cosmonauts were all tragically killed when air leaked out of their spacecraft as they returned to Earth. In 1973, an uncrewed *Salyut 2* space station was launched, but it broke up in orbit.

Space laboratory

◀ **Skylab** *was the first U.S. space laboratory, built inside part of a Saturn V rocket. During the launch, some of the spacecraft's heat shield was damaged. The crew had to cover the damaged area with a shiny sheet to stop their cabin from getting too hot.*

Soviet advances

After *Skylab*, NASA concentrated on developing the space shuttle. Soviet scientists, however, continued to build bigger and better space stations. Between 1974 and 1977, they launched three more spacecraft, *Salyuts 3, 4,* and *5*. These space stations were used mainly as test vehicles, but their crews carried out few experiments.

The problem with space stations up to that point was that the crew's supplies of food, power, water, and air had to be stowed in the space station before the launch. The crews arrived later and could not carry much with them. When the supplies had been exhausted, the space station had to be abandoned.

This problem was solved in 1977, when *Salyut 6* was launched. This space station had two air locks, one at each end of the vehicle. This meant that the

▼ **The Mir** *space station was the largest constructed by the Soviet Union. It took ten years to complete and orbited Earth for 15 years.* **Mir** *suffered from several dangerous accidents, including fires and a collision.*

Skylab

In May 1973, the U.S. National Aeronautics and Space Administration (NASA) abandoned its Apollo missions to the Moon and built its own experimental space station, called *Skylab*. *Skylab* was much bigger than the Salyut space stations. It was adapted from a section of a Saturn V rocket—the rocket used to fly the Apollo craft to the Moon. The fuel tank inside the upper section of rocket was converted into a workshop. An air lock was added, so Apollo spacecraft carrying new three-person crews could dock with the space station.

Skylab was a great success. One of the crews spent 84 days on *Skylab*—a record at the time. The *Skylab* missions were the first to study how the human body changed after extended exposure to the weightlessness environment of space. *Skylab* was also fitted with a telescope used to study the Sun—the most powerful solar telescope ever built.

◀ *The SPACEHAB module is shown in the cargo bay of a space shuttle. It is attached to the crew cabin by a tunnel. SPACEHAB contained a laboratory for studying how the weightlessness environment of space affected the health of the astronauts in space.*

Spacelab

In the 1980s and 1990s, the main U.S. space laboratory was the Spacelab system. This was not a permanent space station that orbited Earth. Instead, Spacelab was carried inside a space shuttle. After completing its experiments, the laboratory was then carried back to Earth.

The Spacelab system was designed by the European Space Agency (ESA). Several European astronauts joined the U.S. shuttle crews to work in Spacelab. Spacelab had a flexible design. Some scientific equipment was fitted inside a large cabin, or module, where astronauts could carry out experiments. The module was connected to the lower crew cabin of the space shuttle by a long tube. The module was designed to be as independent from the rest of the space shuttle as possible. It had a separate life-support system, which kept the air inside clean. However, all of its power was supplied from the space shuttle.

Other Spacelab equipment was carried on a separate pallet. This was outside the module, and the equipment on it was either automatic or had to be operated by an astronaut in a spacesuit. Astronauts could spacewalk to the pallet through a hatch in the roof of the module.

Hard science

The module-pallet system of Spacelab meant that a huge range of experiments could be carried out in space conditions during each shuttle flight. The Soviet space laboratories were most interested in seeing how long people could survive in space. Space scientists needed this information to know if people could make any long journeys to other planets, which could take several years.

Because most shuttle flights lasted for about one week, however, long-lasting experiments were impossible with Spacelab. But a lot of useful information was learned from the Spacelab

crew's Soyuz spacecraft could dock at one end, while an uncrewed supply vessel could dock at the other end. With fresh supplies arriving regularly, crews could stay onboard for much longer. In 1979, two cosmonauts spent a record 175 days inside *Salyut 6*. *Salyut 6* was a huge success. As well as the Soviet Union, crew members from Cuba, Poland, East Germany, and Vietnam took part in missions.

In 1982, *Salyut 7* was launched. This was a copy of *Salyut 6*, and a two-person crew soon increased the record for living in space to 211 days. However, much of *Salyut 7*'s scientific equipment arrived a year later, when an extra section was attached. This second section—called Cosmos—doubled the size of *Salyut 7*. Cosmos also had a large thruster that could be used to move the *Salyut 7* into different positions. Cosmos was only a temporary part of the space station. It was designed to break off from *Salyut 7* and return safely to Earth, carrying used material. In 1985, a second Cosmos section was fitted to the space station.

Despite problems, the crews of *Salyut 7* achieved another first in 1985—an in-space handover. This involved a new crew taking over from the working crew while *Salyut 7* was still in orbit.

▶ *Astronauts perform experiments in Spacelab.*
Spacelab was carried into space in the space shuttle
cargo bay. Experiments were carried out in the
weightless conditions onboard the space station.

missions. Perhaps most importantly, U.S. space scientists figured out how to build, equip, and live in a working space laboratory. This would come in useful when NASA became involved in building a new orbiting space station in the late 1990s.

The Spacelab system was used from 1983 to 1998, after which the SPACEHAB module was introduced. However, the SPACEHAB laboratory was destroyed when the space shuttle *Columbia* broke apart while trying to land in 2003.

Mir

After the success of the Salyut missions, the Soviet Union decided to build a space laboratory made up of several modules. The result was the *Mir* space station. *Mir* was launched in 1986.

Mir's first crew flew over from the *Salyut 7* space station, which they then abandoned. Over the next few years, several modules were added. By the time it was completed in 1996, it was the largest space laboratory ever built. As well as its central crew module, *Mir* had an observatory used to study stars, a laboratory to study the effects of weightlessness on different materials, and two modules to study Earth's environment. These final two modules were added before *Mir* was retired.

Mir had many development problems but proved to be a great success. It was designed to last for just five years but ended up being used for 15 years. From 1989, Mir was continuously occupied by crews for ten years. Most crews stayed in space for six months. However, Soviet cosmonaut and doctor Valery Polyakov (1942–) lived on Mir for 14 months. His record has not yet been broken.

In 1991, the Soviet Union collapsed, and the new Russian government could not afford to develop *Mir* as they had originally planned. To raise money, they made *Mir* available to space scientists from around the world. Different countries paid to have experiments performed on *Mir* by specially trained astronauts and cosmonauts.

In 1995, the U.S. space shuttle *Atlantis* docked with *Mir*. The shuttle brought a new crew to the space station and returned the old crew to Earth. One of the final *Mir* modules was also carried into space by *Atlantis*. This was the beginning of cooperation between NASA, the Russian Space Agency, and other space agencies around the world to build the International Space Station.

International Space Station

In 2001, an empty *Mir* had completed its mission and was allowed to plunge toward, and burn up in, Earth's atmosphere. However, another space station was already under construction. In 1998, the first modules of the International Space Station (ISS) were connected by shuttle astronauts. The ISS has a similar design to *Mir*, with several modules connected to a central crew module. Modules are being built in Europe, Japan, and Brazil, as well as Russia and the United States. The ISS is continuing research into the effects of weightlessness.

The ISS is already the largest artificial object in space, having as much room inside as two jumbo jets. It can even be seen in the night's sky. The ISS was due for completion in 2003, but delays have put back this date to around 2010.

See also: ROCKET • SPACE PROBE •
SPACE SHUTTLE • TELESCOPE

Space probe

A space probe is a robotic machine sent from Earth to explore other celestial objects. Probes take close-up pictures of planets and their moons. Some even make soft landings on the surfaces of other planets and send back data about rocks and soils.

The first space probes were sent to the Moon because the Moon is the nearest body to Earth. Since then, space probes have visited all the planets except Pluto. Others have landed on moons and asteroids and have flown through the tails of comets. Many of the oldest probes have left the solar system and are now speeding toward the stars and out of range of the most powerful radios. Even if scientists could keep in contact with these probes, they would have a long wait. A probe would take 100,000 years to reach the nearest star to Earth.

A space probe carries instruments on board that study the places it visits and send back data to scientists on Earth. One of the most useful instruments on a probe is a camera, although not all space probes carry cameras. Other instruments are used for measuring magnetic fields and particles in space and for studying the temperature and makeup of bodies that the probe encounters.

Space probes need electricity to power their instruments. Probes that are traveling near the Sun are fitted with solar cells that turn light into electricity. Space probes that spend long periods in darkness or are traveling far away from the Sun carry small nuclear power plants that produce their own supply of electricity.

▶ *The Cassini probe is tested before being launched in 1997. The probe carried a smaller spacecraft called Huygens, which became the first space probe to land on the surface of Titan—Saturn's largest moon. Huygens discovered a muddy world shrouded in a fog of methane gas.*

To direct a probe over millions of miles requires accurate knowledge of the scale of the solar system. Scientists use the gravity of the planets to fling probes at great speeds across space. Each probe is equipped with a small rocket that can adjust the probe's course during the trip if necessary.

All the data collected by the probe are turned into radio signals and sent back to Earth. The faint signals are picked up by giant, dish-shaped radio receivers on Earth. The National Aeronautics and Space Administration (NASA) has a network of three deep-space tracking stations around the world that keeps them in touch with distant spacecraft. Each station has two dishes for sending and receiving data. One dish is 85 feet (26 meters) in diameter, and the other is 210 feet (64 meters) in diameter. The receivers can pick up signals sent from beyond the edge of the solar system.

Probes to the Moon

The first successful space probe was the Soviet *Luna 2*, which flew into the Moon on September 14, 1959. Launched on October 4, 1959, *Luna 3* flew behind the Moon and sent back the first pictures of its dark side. This had never been seen before because the Moon always keeps the same face turned toward Earth. The pictures showed a rugged landscape. On February 3, 1966, another Soviet probe, *Luna 9*, made the first soft landing on the Moon's surface. It sent back pictures of the surface.

Before sending astronauts to the Moon, NASA scouted ahead with probes. Several *Surveyor* probes landed all over the Moon to confirm that the crust was strong enough to support the weight of a lander. The *Lunar Orbiter* probes photographed the Moon in great detail.

Soviet scientists did not send people to the Moon but explored the Moon's surface with remote-controlled vehicles. Their *Luna 16* probe landed on the Moon on September 12, 1970, and collected lunar rocks, which were sent back to Earth.

▲ *NASA technicians inspect the **Pioneer 3** probe before its launch in 1958. The probe was meant to study radiation in Earth's outer atmosphere, but its launch rocket did not attain the required altitude.*

MAJOR SPACE PROBES (listed chronologically by launch date)		
Probe	Date launched	Accomplishment
Luna 2	September 12, 1959	First probe to reach the Moon—September 14, 1959
Mariner 2	August 27, 1962	First probe to pass Venus—December 14, 1962
Mariner 4	November 28, 1964	First probe to pass Mars—July 14, 1965
Luna 9	January 31, 1966	First probe to soft land on the Moon—February 3, 1966
Venera 7	August 17, 1970	First probe to land on Venus—December 15, 1970
Pioneer 10	March 3, 1972	First probe to pass Jupiter—December 3, 1973
Pioneer 11	April 6, 1973	First probe to pass Saturn—September 1, 1979
Mariner 10	November 3, 1973	First probe to pass Mercury—March 29, 1974
Viking 1	August 20, 1975	Mars orbiter and lander—June 19, 1976
Voyager 2	August 20, 1977	First probe to pass Uranus (January 24, 1986) and Neptune (August 25, 1989)
Giotto	July 2, 1986	First probe to Comet Halley—March 13, 1986
Galileo	October 18, 1989	Sent probe into Jupiter's atmosphere—December 7, 1995
NEAR	February 17, 1996	First probe to land on an asteroid—February 12, 2000
Cassini	October 15, 1997	Landed miniprobe *Huygens* on Titan—January 14, 2005
Spirit	June 10, 2003	Mars exploration rover landed on Mars—January 3, 2004
Opportunity	July 7, 2003	Mars exploration rover landed on Mars—January 25, 2004

Probes to Venus and Mercury

The first space probe to reach another planet was NASA's *Mariner 2,* which went within 22,000 miles (35,000 kilometers) of Venus on December 14, 1962. Astronomers had never seen the surface of Venus because it is permanently hidden behind thick clouds. Light reflecting off the clouds makes Venus the brightest object in the sky after the Sun and Moon. Because Venus is between Earth and the Sun, it is often seen at dawn and dusk and therefore is often called the morning or evening star.

Mariner 2 discovered that Venus was incredibly hot and not at all similar to Earth. A series of Soviet probes then plunged into Venus's atmosphere. One by one they were roasted and crushed by the planet's atmosphere. At last, on December 15, 1970, *Venera 7* made it to the surface and survived there for 23 minutes before it, too, succumbed to the extreme conditions. *Venera 7* found that the surface of the planet was a staggering 890°F (475°C), and the atmosphere pressed down nearly one hundred times more than the air on Earth.

Later, Soviet probes sent back photographs from the surface, showing a rocky landscape bathed in orange light. In 1978, several U.S. probes plunged into the atmosphere of Venus, sampling its thick clouds of sulfuric acid (H_2SO_4). Another NASA probe, called *Pioneer Venus Orbiter,* went into orbit around Venus on December 4, 1978, mapping the surface beneath the clouds using radar. The instruments continued to gather data until the spacecraft burned up in Venus's atmosphere on October 8, 1992.

The innermost planet is Mercury. On March 29, 1974, NASA's *Mariner 10* took a first look at this planet. Mariner passed 460 miles (750 kilometers) from Mercury. Mercury turned out to be a cratered ball of rock that resembles Earth's Moon.

▶ **Voyager 2 *was launched on August 20, 1977—16 days before* Voyager 1. *However,* Voyager 2 *arrived at its first rendezvous with Jupiter in July 1979—about four months later than* Voyager 1. Voyager 2 *left the solar system in 1989, but it still sends information back to Earth. It is thought that* Voyager 2 *will continue working until at least 2020.***

◀ *This image of Saturn's rings was taken by* **Voyager 2** *in 1981, when the probe was 1.7 million miles (2.7 million kilometers) from the planet. The rings are 170,000 miles (270,000 kilometers) wide but less than 324 feet (100 meters) thick.*

Life on Mars

Mars is the most studied of planets in the solar system after Earth. The first space probe passed the planet on July 14, 1965. *Mariner 4* sent back images of craters dotting the planet's sandy surface. Many scientists were disappointed. They expected to find signs of life on Mars. Whereas Venus had turned out to be hot, Mars was a dry, frozen world.

From 1971 to 1972, *Mariner 9* surveyed the planet from orbit, revealing giant volcanoes and signs of what seemed to be dried-up rivers and lakes. Astronomers began to think that perhaps the climate on Mars had been wetter in the past, and life had existed there then. Two Viking probes were sent to find out more. Each came in two halves—an orbiter to survey the planet and a lander equipped with video cameras, a weather station, and a device to analyze the planet's soil.

The *Viking 1* lander touched down in a lowland plain on June 19, 1976. Its cameras showed a rock-strewn red desert, without any sign of plants or animals. On September 3, 1976, *Viking 2*'s lander came down at a spot on the opposite side of the

planet. Even though it was midsummer on Mars, air temperatures reached only –20°F (–29°C) in the afternoon, falling to –65°F (–85°C) at night.

Each Viking lander scooped up several samples of Martian soil and put them in incubators that would make any microscopic bugs in the soil grow quickly. The results were negative. At neither landing site did the Viking landers find any definite sign of even the simplest living matter.

Space probes returned to Mars in the 1990s and in the early twenty-first century, but several accidents occurred. NASA's *Mars Observer* was launched in October 1992 but failed to enter orbit around the planet. Launched on December 4, 1996, *Mars Pathfinder*, another largely U.S. mission, was much more successful. On July 4, 1997, the probe's lander arrived safely on the surface. The lander carried a rover named *Sojourner*, which spent more than two months exploring the landing site, sending back information about the Martian rocks. A Soviet mission to Mars failed that same year, and two more NASA missions were lost over the next two years.

▶ *This picture of Neptune was taken by* **Voyager 2** *from 4.4 million miles (7 million kilometers) away. The Great Dark Spot—a storm system in Neptune's atmosphere—is at the center of the picture. At the bottom left is a pale feature called Scooter.*

▶ *The Mars rovers* **Spirit** *and* **Opportunity** *studied the rocks and soil on the surface of Mars. They were looking for signs of water and anything that might have been produced by living things.*

On June 2, 2003, the European Space Agency (ESA) and NASA launched *Mars Express.* Like the Viking probes, this spacecraft had an orbiter and a lander. The orbiter studied the Martian atmosphere, but the lander, *Beagle 2* (named for the ship that carried English naturalist Charles Darwin), never made contact with Earth once it touched down on Mars.

A few months later, in January 2004, NASA's Mars exploration rovers, named *Spirit* and *Opportunity,* landed safely on the planet. Compared to earlier Mars rovers, they were huge—about the size of golf carts. As well as sending back pictures, the rovers were designed to look for signs of water on the surface of Mars by analyzing rocks and soil in great detail. They even had drills to penetrate beneath the ground.

Distant giants

Beyond Mars, the solar system is home to five more planets and countless comets and asteroids. Probes have visited all of these outer planets except Pluto—the smallest and most distant from the Sun. These probes spent many years reaching their destination and are now heading into deep space. The first to set out on this interplanetary marathon

was *Pioneer 10* on March 3, 1972. It was boosted to an unprecedented top speed of 31,000 miles (50,000 kilometers) per hour. *Pioneer 10* swung past Jupiter on December 3, 1973, giving astronomers their first close-up look at the solar system's largest planet. Its mission accomplished, *Pioneer 10* drifted off into space, eventually leaving the solar system entirely in June 1983. This mission was followed on April 6, 1974 by *Pioneer 11*, which took the first close-up look at the ringed planet Saturn on September 1, 1979.

NASA's more advanced Voyager probes followed the Pioneer missions. *Voyager 1* was launched on September 5, 1977. It reached Jupiter on March 5, 1979. The giant planet's gravity swung *Voyager 1* around and flung it toward Saturn. The probe flew by this planet on November 12, 1980, before flying out of the solar system. *Voyager 2* had a longer journey. It was launched on August 20, 1977, but traveled more slowly than its sister probe. It did not arrive at Jupiter until July 9, 1979. It, too, was then swung toward Saturn, arriving there on August 15, 1981. The Voyager missions studied not only these two planets, but also their moons. Several of these

▲ *The Mars exploration rovers sent back the most detailed images of Mars's surface ever taken. This one taken by* **Spirit** *showed that Mars is like a desert on Earth. Strong winds blow red dust into the atmosphere making the sky pink.*

are large enough to be regarded as worlds in their own right. One of Jupiter's moons, called Io, was discovered to have volcanoes that erupt with sulfur. Saturn's largest moon, Titan, was seen to be a frozen world similar to Earth.

Instead of leaving the solar system, *Voyager 2* was redirected by Saturn's gravity toward Uranus. It flew past this planet on January 24, 1986. Then the probe traveled on to Neptune, arriving there on August 25, 1989. As well as sending back close-up pictures of these two giant icy planets, *Voyager 2* discovered several previously unknown moons and three rings around Neptune. Beyond Neptune, *Voyager 2* traveled out of the solar system. However, it is still sending back information about the Sun's magnetic field. In case they encounter any kind of life, the Voyager probes carry pictures of humans and a vinyl record with sounds from Earth.

In the 1990s, the *Galileo Orbiter* returned to Jupiter. This spacecraft was launched by shuttle *Atlantis* on October 18, 1989. *Galileo* traveled past Venus and flew back past Earth before finally going into orbit around Jupiter in December 1995. It released a probe that fell into Jupiter's atmosphere on December 7, 1995. The atmospheric probe sent back information for nearly an hour before being destroyed by heat and pressure. *Galileo* studied Jupiter and its moons Io and Europa for four years, eventually plunging into Jupiter's atmosphere on September 21, 2003.

On July 1, 2004, *Cassini*, run by both NASA and ESA, became the first spacecraft to orbit Saturn. It has flown close to many of Saturn's moons and rings. On January 14, 2005, *Huygens,* a probe carried to Saturn by *Cassini,* landed on Titan.

Comets and asteroids

The solar system is also home to many comets and asteroids. Comets are lumps of ice and rock that come from the very edge of the solar system. As they approach the Sun, they develop a glowing tail of gas. On July 4, 2005, the *Deep Impact* probe collided with comet Tempel 1. Scientists hoped to learn more about the composition of the solar system from the results of the collision.

Asteroids are rocks left over from the formation of planets. Most are found in a belt between Mars and Jupiter. *Galileo* discovered the first asteroid on its way to Jupiter. *Near-Earth Asteroid Rendezvous (NEAR)* became the first probe to land on an asteroid, called Eros, on February 12, 2000.

See also: ROCKET • SATELLITE • SOLAR ENERGY • SOLAR SYSTEM • SPACE LABORATORY

Space shuttle

The space shuttle is the first reusable spacecraft. It is part rocket and part airplane. On the launching pad, it stands about 18 stories high and is designed to go up into space like a rocket. However, the shuttle flies back to Earth and lands like an airplane.

The space shuttle is the world's first reusable spacecraft. It was developed by NASA, the U.S. National Aeronautics and Space Administration, in the 1970s. The formal name for the space shuttle is the Space Transportation System (STS).

The first shuttle to travel into space was *Columbia*. It was launched on April 12, 1981. Since then, a total of five space shuttles have carried out more than one hundred missions in space. Shuttles carry out a variety of useful roles in space. These include launching satellites and carrying space-science laboratories into orbit. Shuttle astronauts also repair faulty and damaged satellites and are helping assemble the International Space Station.

As well as *Columbia*, the shuttles were named *Challenger*, *Discovery*, *Atlantis*, and *Endeavor*. All these spacecraft share their names with the ships of famous explorers. (A Soviet space shuttle named *Buran*, meaning "snowstorm," was launched for an uncrewed flight in 1988, but it never flew again.)

In two separate accidents, both *Challenger* and *Columbia* have been destroyed, killing both their crews. *Challenger* blew up shortly after takeoff in 1986, while *Columbia* broke apart when reentering Earth's atmosphere in 2003.

Planning the space shuttle

As its Apollo program, which took astronauts to the Moon, came to an end in 1972, NASA realized that space travel was becoming very expensive. In the same year, the U.S. Congress asked NASA to develop a reusable spaceplane that would make

▲ Space shuttle **Columbia** *lifts off in October 1993. The spacecraft is powered into space by its own three rocket engines and two large boosters, which are attached to a giant central fuel tank.*

crewed space flight much cheaper. The result of this development program was the space shuttle. Shuttles have been carrying U.S. astronauts ever since.

The STS launch system consists of a winged orbiter, which most people call the shuttle, a pair of rocket boosters, and a giant external fuel tank. The

THE SHUTTLE ORBITER

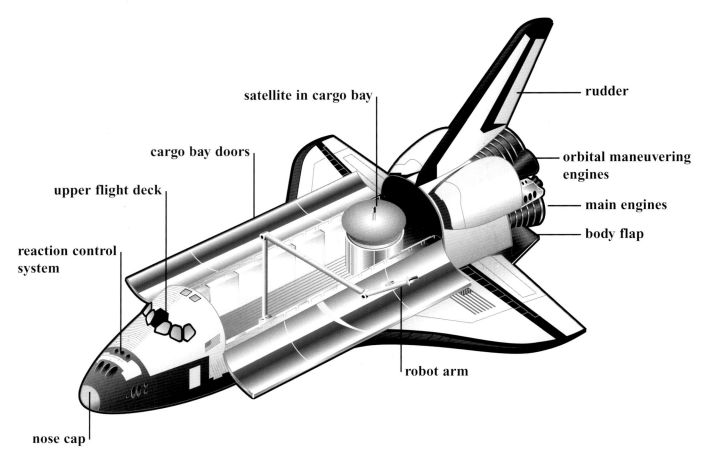

satellite in cargo bay

rudder

cargo bay doors

orbital maneuvering engines

upper flight deck

main engines

reaction control system

body flap

nose cap

robot arm

boosters and tank are used only during takeoff. At the edge of space, they fall back to Earth. Only the orbiter, or shuttle, makes it into orbit.

The shuttle is about 120 feet (37.2 meters) long, a little smaller than a 737 airliner. Its wingspan is 78 feet (23.8 meters). The pilots' cabin, or flight deck, is in the shuttle's nose, as in an ordinary airplane. Below the flight deck are the crew's living quarters, sleeping bunks, and an air-flushed toilet. As well as the pilots, shuttle crews also include scientists, engineers, and other specialists. Half the shuttle's length is taken up by a cargo bay, which can carry 32 tons (29 tonnes) into orbit and bring about half that weight back to Earth.

Power for the shuttle

The shuttle has three rocket engines mounted at the rear. During launch, the engines' liquid fuel is fed from the external tank strapped to the underside of the shuttle. The rocket boosters are attached to the side of the fuel tank. These are powered by solid fuel.

▲ *Half the length of the 122-foot (37-meter) shuttle orbiter is taken up by its cargo, or payload, bay. Often, companies pay for the shuttle to carry and launch their satellites. This money helps pay for other space shuttle missions.*

DID YOU KNOW?

Two space shuttles have been destroyed during their missions. In January 1986, *Challenger* exploded just 73 seconds after liftoff. Cold weather had caused a leak in one of the rocket boosters, which burned a hole in the fuel tank, causing an immense explosion. All seven crew members were killed. In February 2003, *Columbia* broke apart above Texas about 15 minutes before it was due to land. It was discovered that a piece of insulation had fallen off the fuel tank during liftoff and had pierced a hole in the shuttle's wing.

SHUTTLE TAKEOFF AND LANDING SEQUENCES

4. The external tank separates before the shuttle enters orbit. The shuttle orbits upside down.

3. The main engines cut off after 8½ minutes.

2. The solid rocket boosters are exhausted and jettisoned after 2 minutes.

1. The two solid rocket boosters and main engines fire on takeoff.

Takeoff Sequence

Landing Sequence

1. The shuttle uses its maneuvering engines to slow down and position itself for reentry.

2. The heat-resistant tiles protect the shuttle from the heat produced as it reenters the atmosphere.

3. With the shuttle behaving like a glider, the pilot makes turns to slow its descent.

4. The space shuttle commander uses radar-controlled visual aids to position the shuttle for landing.

5. The shuttle lands on a long runway.

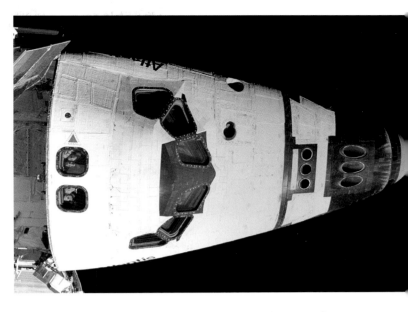

▲ *Shuttle astronauts look out of the windows in the roof of the flight deck. The circular holes in the shuttle's nose are part of the in-space steering system.*

The shuttle also has two small engines in the tail, called orbital maneuvering engines. These are used to steer it into orbit and adjust the course. In the craft's nose and tail there are small gas jets that also help the pilots steer the spacecraft when in orbit.

Liftoff

The space shuttle is launched like a rocket. Its three engines are the first to fire, followed by the two solid-fuel boosters. Together, they produce an upward thrust of 7 million pounds (3.1 million kilograms), which is enough to lift everything off the ground and reach the altitude required for orbit.

About two minutes after liftoff, the two solid-fuel booster rockets are released, and they return to Earth by parachute. At this point, the shuttle is traveling at 17,000 miles (27,300 kilometers) per hour. Eight and one-half minutes after lift-off, an explosive charge spins the huge fuel tank away from the spacecraft. It is shattered to pieces and burns up in Earth's atmosphere.

The cargo bay

Once in orbit, the shuttle's cargo bay faces toward Earth. The bay is 60 feet (18.3 meters) long by 15 feet (4.6 meters) wide. It has room for several satellites to be carried at once, and it sometimes also carries a laboratory module. When in orbit, the doors of the cargo bay are opened by the crew. This helps release some of the heat that has built up inside the orbiter during its journey into space.

In space, the contents of the cargo bay are moved around with a remote-controlled robotic arm. The arm is controlled at the aft station at the rear of the flight deck. The arm is equipped with a video camera that sends pictures to a screen at the aft station to help the crew control it. The arm picks up satellites and releases them into orbit. In some cases, the satellites are plucked from orbit by the arm and stowed in the cargo bay so they can be repaired or carried back to Earth. The robot arm is also used to hold equipment, such as telescopes, clear of the spacecraft while they perform their tasks. Astronauts in space suits are also carried around the cargo bay by the arm.

Servicing space stations

During the last ten years, one of the main missions performed by shuttle crews has been related to space stations. In 1995, shuttle *Atlantis* docked with the Russian space station *Mir*. The shuttle carried a

▶ *The cargo bay of shuttle* **Discovery** *contains the SPACEHAB laboratory. This space-science module at the rear of the cargo bay is connected to the shuttle's cabin by a long tunnel.* **Discovery** *has since been used to test safety measures put in place after the* **Columbia** *disaster in 2003 and to resupply the International Space Station.*

▲ *Space shuttle* **Atlantis** *docked with* **Mir,** *the Russian space station, in 1995. The shuttle carried a new crew of cosmonauts—Russian astronauts—to the space station. Mir was abandoned in 2001, and its controllers crashed it into the Pacific Ocean.*

new Russian crew to the space station and ferried the previous crew back to Earth. A new docking system had to be fitted to the shuttle, so it could connect to *Mir's* door safely. During the next five years, NASA astronauts joined the Russian crews to learn about living on a space station.

In 1998, NASA and other space agencies from around the world began to build the International Space Station (ISS). The shuttles are being used to carry many of the station's modules into space. The 2005 *Discovery* mission to the ISS was the first since the *Columbia* disaster. During the launch, debris falling from the fuel tank damaged part of *Discovery's* nose section. The damage was repaired during one of three spacewalks.

Returning to Earth

On its return to Earth, the shuttle is first swung around, so it is orbiting backward. Its main engines are fired briefly to slow the spacecraft. The pilot then flips the shuttle over as it begins to plunge downward into the atmosphere. The friction of the air rushing past the spacecraft causes the shuttle to

heat up to 2700°F (1482°C). The shuttle's nose must be kept at the correct angle, so only the craft's underside gets hot. The underside and other exposed parts are protected by 30,000 lightweight heat-resistant silica tiles. Without the tiles, the metal parts of the shuttle would begin to melt, and the weakened spacecraft would break apart.

As it drops below 75 miles (127 kilometers), thicker air allows the shuttle to handle more like an airplane. Because it has no engine power, the pilot must glide the shuttle even though it is traveling at 12,500 miles (20,000 kilometers) per hour. The air slows the shuttle down, and at 70,000 feet (21,350 meters) the speed is down to about 400 miles (644 kilometers) per hour. The shuttle touches down on the runway at 215 miles (346 kilometers) per hour, and it is slowed to a stop by a large parachute.

See also: SPACE LABORATORY •
SPACE PROBE • SPACE SUIT

▲ *The shuttle* **Atlantis** *touches down at the Kennedy Space Center in Florida. The shuttle also sometimes lands at Edwards Air Force Base in California. There are also several emergency landing sites around the world if the crew cannot get back to the United States.*

▼ *A technician cuts a heat-resistant tile before gluing it to a space shuttle by hand. The tiles protect the spacecraft from the very high temperatures produced as they fly back into Earth's atmosphere.*

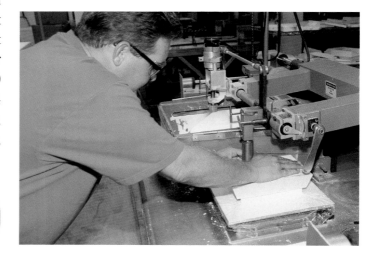

Space suit

A space suit has to be worn when an astronaut leaves a spacecraft. The space suit keeps the astronaut warm, supplies air for breathing, protects the astronaut against space debris such as rocks, and even contains a bag of water so the astronaut can have a drink whenever he or she needs one.

When astronauts exit a spacecraft, they need to have almost as much protection and support as they have in the safety of the spacecraft. For this reason, the space suit is sometimes called the "human-powered spacecraft."

Why is a space suit needed?

The environment in space is extremely harsh. There is no air to breathe, nor is there any pressure, and body fluids would quickly boil away. It is either very cold or very hot, and astronauts run the constant risk of being hit by tiny particles, called micro-meteoroids, that move through space at high speed. Without a complex space suit to protect them in space, astronauts would very soon die. A space suit is not just one suit but has a number of different layers, sometimes more than 20. (The inner and outer layers will be discussed below and on the following pages.)

The inner suit

The astronaut first puts on the liquid cooling and ventilation garment. This is an elastic, one-piece suit worn next to the skin and zipped up at the front. It has ventilation holes in it so that air can reach the skin, and a network of tubes that carry cooling water to keep the astronaut cool when carrying out tough physical jobs. Socks of the same material cover the feet and attach to the main suit.

A urine-collection bag is strapped to the astronaut's groin underneath the cooling and ventilation garment, and a bag of drinking water is attached to the main body of the garment.

▶ *Anchored to a foot restraint on the Space Station Remote Manipulator System (SSRMS) and wearing his extravehicular mobility unit (EMU) space suit, astronaut David A. Wolf installs a camera on the International Space Station.*

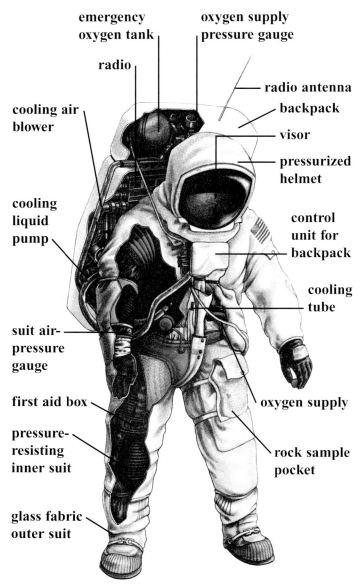

emergency oxygen tank

oxygen supply pressure gauge

radio

radio antenna

cooling air blower

backpack

visor

pressurized helmet

cooling liquid pump

control unit for backpack

cooling tube

suit air-pressure gauge

first aid box

pressure-resisting inner suit

glass fabric outer suit

oxygen supply

rock sample pocket

▲ *This illustration shows the type of space suit worn by U.S. astronauts during the Apollo missions to the Moon. The suit includes more than 20 layers and has a backpack that contains oxygen, cooling-liquid supply equipment, and a radio.*

Headgear

Next, the astronaut puts on tight-fitting headgear, which carries headphones and a microphone so that the astronaut can communicate with the rest of the crew and the National Aeronautics and Space Administration (NASA) control on Earth. This system is also linked to warning devices. If anything goes wrong with the space suit or the backpack, a steady tone is heard in the headphones, warning the astronaut of the problem.

The outer suit

Once the inner and outer suits are connected, the astronaut then steps into the bottom half of the outer suit. This covers the feet, legs, and bottom half of the body.

The astronaut then wriggles into the top half of the suit—head first—and the two halves are joined by fasteners around a circular metal ring to provide an airtight seal. The gloves and helmet are attached to the suit in the same way.

This outer suit is tough enough to protect against high-speed micrometeoroids, cosmic radiation, and rubbing against Moon rocks or the spacecraft. The outer suit is also flexible enough to allow the astronaut to move around freely.

▼ *Assistants help space shuttle astronaut Story Musgrave put on his space suit. He is preparing to enter a vacuum chamber and rehearse repairs to the Hubble Space Telescope.*

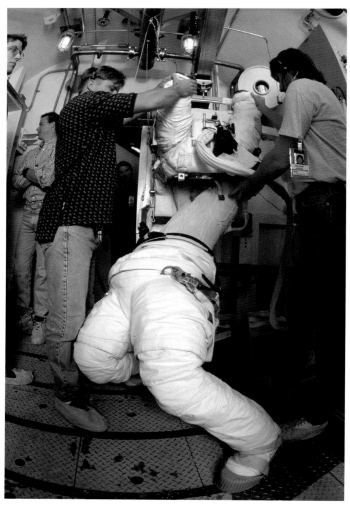

◄ *Astronaut Christer Fuglesang wears a training version of the extravehicular mobility unit space suit during an underwater simulation of extravehicular activity.*

Life support

The backpack is the astronaut's life-support system. It is fairly heavy, weighing around 160 pounds (73 kilograms), but in the weightless conditions of space it is not too much for the astronaut to bear. The main functions of the backpack are to provide oxygen to breathe, remove waste carbon dioxide and water vapor, maintain the space suit at a fixed temperature, and keep the astronaut in contact with the spacecraft.

Breathing

Oxygen from the backpack enters the space suit through the helmet at the back and flows forward and down the body. Oxygen is breathed in by the astronaut, and carbon dioxide is exhaled along with water vapor, which is also produced by sweating.

All these gases are removed from the suit by the cooling garment at holes near the feet and wrists. From there, the air returns to the backpack, where it is filtered to remove the carbon dioxide and any dust and odors. It is cooled in a machine called a sublimator (that works in a similar way to a refrigerator) and returned to the suit.

Temperature control

The temperature of the space suit is set by the astronaut. It is maintained by the cooled water passing through the cooling undergarment from the backpack. The water is cooled in the sublimator. The undergarment can easily remove the heat and sweat produced by the hardest-working astronaut.

The backpack carries the radio and enough oxygen and cooling water for seven hours of extravehicular activity (EVA). There is even a reserve pack with a 30-minute supply of oxygen if the main backpack fails.

The reusable suit

For more recent space shuttle missions, astronauts have been issued with one-size space suits—the only parts made to different sizes are the gloves and boots. This means that the space suits are built to fit any astronaut. Just like the shuttle itself, they have been designed to last for several years and to be used and reused by a number of people.

See also: SPACE LABORATORY • SPACE SHUTTLE

Speaker

A loudspeaker changes electrical signals into sound. Developed during the 1920s, the moving coil loudspeaker is the most common type now used. Modern loudspeakers are mounted in cabinets, and much attention is given to the quality of the sound.

Early record players reproduced sound by mechanical means. The vibrations of a needle on grooves pressed into a vinyl disk were transmitted directly to a horn on the playing arm of the record player. By the 1920s, transducers—devices for converting electricity into another form of energy—had been invented. One of these was the electrical pickup, which converted the mechanical signals from a record player needle (the stylus) into electrical signals that could be amplified by a vacuum tube. However, some method of converting the electrical signals into sound was needed, and the first "hornless" loudspeakers began to appear.

The most important work in developing loudspeakers was done by U.S. scientists Chester W. Rice and Edward W. Kellogg. They used a moving coil hung between the poles of a magnet to change electrical signals into mechanical vibrations. This idea was not new—it had been used in a device called a "bellowing telephone," which was invented by English physicist Oliver Lodge (1851–1940) in 1898. However, the loudspeaker system devised by Rice and Kellogg is still used now. Its simple construction and quality of performance are unlikely to be improved upon.

▼ *Headphones are miniature loudspeakers held over the ear by a band or wire worn on the head. People often use headphones when they want to listen to music without disturbing other people or when levels of surrounding noise are high.*

The moving-coil loudspeaker

The main parts of a moving-coil loudspeaker are a diaphragm made from plastic or strengthened paper, a permanent magnet, and a coil of wire called the voice coil. The diaphragm is hung from a metal frame by springy extensions around its edge and at its center. Attached to the center of the diaphragm is a cylindrical tube, called the former, around which lies the voice coil. The former and the voice coil are placed between the poles of a permanent magnet.

When an electrical current passes through the voice coil, a magnetic field is induced. This magnetic field interacts with the magnetic field of the permanent magnet, which makes the voice coil and former move. The current produced by an electrical pickup varies, and the coil and tube vibrate in relation to these variations. The vibrations are passed on to the diaphragm, which generates sound waves in the air.

Enclosures, woofers, and tweeters

The human ear can hear frequencies of between 30 hertz (low pitch) and more than 16,000 hertz (high pitch). To get a loudspeaker system to reproduce both low and high frequencies equally well poses certain problems. First, low-pitched sounds coming from the back of a speaker tend to cancel out those coming from the front. This problem can be overcome by placing the speaker in a cabinet (enclosure) and packing it with sound-proofing material. In other designs, the cabinet is "tuned" so that the sounds from the back of the speaker enhance those from the front.

Another problem is that high-pitched sounds are not radiated (sent out) in all directions. Instead, they become concentrated in a narrow beam. This effect is more noticeable with large diaphragms. To overcome this problem, two (or more) speakers are used in the same cabinet. A large speaker, called a woofer, reproduces low-pitched sounds, and a smaller speaker, called a tweeter, reproduces high-pitched notes. These notes are fed from an electrical filter, or crossover circuit, which sends the right signals to each speaker.

MOVING-COIL LOUDSPEAKER

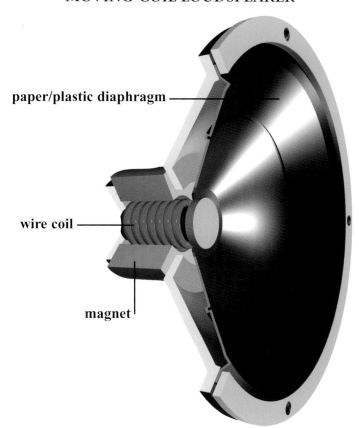

paper/plastic diaphragm

wire coil

magnet

▲ *The moving-coil loudspeaker turns an electrical signal into pressure waves that are heard as sound.*

Other loudspeakers

Certain other types of loudspeakers are also available. A ribbon loudspeaker can be used to reproduce high-pitched notes. The ribbon loudspeaker has a light, metal ribbon in place of the moving coil, which also acts as the diaphragm. In an electrostatic loudspeaker, the diaphragm is a light metal plate held between two perforated (punched with holes) fixed plates. A high voltage is connected between the diaphragm and one of the fixed plates, and the signal is applied, by way of an isolating transformer, across the fixed plates. The signal causes a variation in the electrostatic forces between the fixed plate and the diaphragm, which then vibrates. This type of loudspeaker works well at all but very low frequencies.

See also: SOUND • SOUND RECORDING

Specific gravity

Specific gravity, or relative density, is a measure of the density of a substance. The practical uses of measuring the specific gravity of substances are wide-ranging. Measuring the specific gravity of the liquid in a lead-acid battery, for example, can show if it needs recharging. Specific gravity can also reveal the strength of alcoholic drinks.

When people think about a densely packed crowd in a football stadium, they probably imagine a lot of people in the crowd, all tightly packed together. In the same way, when people talk about a dense material, they mean that the atoms and molecules that make up the material are closely packed together.

A metal such as gold is denser than aluminum. A piece of gold feels heavier and has more mass than a similar-sized piece of aluminum. The important idea here is that equal volumes of the two materials

▶ *Two geologists use a gravity meter inside a cave at Bowling Green, Kentucky. The recordings will provide a map of the locations of tunnels to drill wells that will vent toxic fumes away from groundwater.*

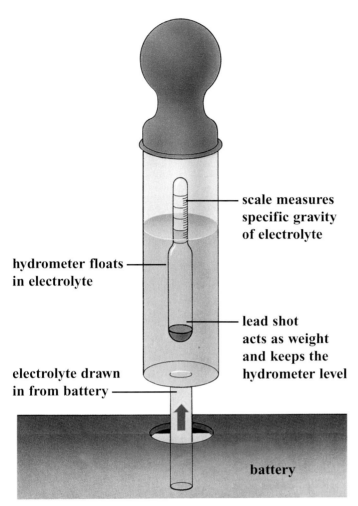

scale measures
specific gravity
of electrolyte

hydrometer floats
in electrolyte

lead shot
acts as weight
and keeps the
hydrometer level

electrolyte drawn
in from battery

battery

▲ *Hydrometers can be used to measure the specific gravity of liquid electrolyte in a lead-acid battery.*

should be measured. The density is therefore a measure of the mass of a standard volume of a substance, and it is usually measured in kilograms per cubic meter. For example, 1 cubic meter of gold has a mass of 19,300 kilograms (42,550 pounds), but the same volume of aluminum has a mass of 2,700 kilograms (5,950 pounds).

Relative measurement

Another way of measuring density is to compare the mass of a volume of a material with the same volume of water under standard conditions. This measurement is the specific gravity, or relative density, and it does not have units because it is a ratio of the two masses. For example, the specific gravity of gold is 19.3, so gold is 19.3 times denser than water. It is important to note that the specific

gravity is always numerically the same as the density in grams per cubic centimeter because the density of water under standard conditions is close to 1 gram per cubic centimeter.

Archimedes

Greek scholar Archimedes (c. 287–212 BCE) demonstrated the first practical use for measuring specific gravity. Hiero II (c. 308–216 BCE), the ruler of Syracuse, Greece, asked Archimedes to find out if his crown was pure gold, or if the goldsmith had cheated by adding some silver. Archimedes struck upon the answer while taking a bath. When he got into the bath, water flowed over the edge. He realized that the volume of water that flowed out must be equal to his volume. So, if two objects with the same mass were put into the water, the denser object would displace less water than the other. He then showed that the crown displaced more water than the same mass of gold, proving that the goldsmith had cheated Hiero. Legend has it that when Archimedes discovered the principle of displacement, he ran through the streets of Syracuse shouting Eureka! ("I have found it!").

Measuring the specific gravity of liquids

An instrument called a hydrometer is used to measure the specific gravity of liquids. This device consists of a float made of a glass bulb weighted with lead shot, with a long, narrow neck that rises above the surface of the liquid to be measured. When the hydrometer is immersed in different liquids, it displaces the same weight of liquid equal to the weight of the hydrometer itself. Therefore the volume of liquid displaced depends on the specific gravity of the liquid.

Hydrometers of this type are used to measure the liquid electrolyte in lead-acid batteries. When fully charged, the electrolyte has a specific gravity of 1.28, but this decreases as the battery is discharged. Hydrometers are also used to measure the alcohol content of beer, wine, and liquor.

See *also*: MASS AND WEIGHT • METAL

Spectroscopy

A rainbow forms in the sky when sunlight shines through raindrops. The water acts as a prism, and the different colors of white light are separated into the pattern of red, orange, yellow, green, blue, indigo, and violet. This is known as a spectrum. Spectroscopy is the study of spectra, and it is used to figure out where the light came from and how it was produced.

▲ *Technicians prepare a space telescope for loading onto a space shuttle. The telescope contains two spectrographs that detect ultraviolet light emitted by stars. The information it collects is used to find out how stars evolve and produce light and heat.*

Light is a form of electromagnetic radiation. Most radiation, such as heat, microwaves, and X-rays, is invisible, but it behaves in the same way as visible light. All radiation has a wavelength and frequency. The wavelength is the distance it takes for the wave to complete one cycle—from one peak to the next. The frequency is a measure of how many waves occur every second.

The electromagnetic spectrum

In a vacuum, all radiation travels at the speed of light (186,000 miles or 300,000 kilometers per second). Therefore, the longer the wavelength, the lower the frequency. Radiation with a short wavelength has more waves in the same amount of time as radiation with a longer wavelength.

When waves are arranged in order of wavelength, they create a spectrum (*plural*, spectra). The wavelengths of visible light are just one part of the electromagnetic spectrum. It is called visible light because the eyes can detect the waves. Other forms of electromagnetic radiation have longer and shorter wavelengths that people cannot detect in the same way. For example, radiation that has wavelengths a little longer than visible light is called infrared. The body detects infrared radiation as heat. Below infrared in the spectrum, radiation takes the form of microwaves. This is the radiation used to cook food in microwave ovens, to communicate using cell phones, and to broadcast programs on the radio and television. Radiation with the longest wavelengths is called radio waves.

Radiation with shorter wavelengths than visible light is called ultraviolet light. This is produced by fluorescent lamps—so-called "black lights." Ultraviolet radiation in sunlight causes sunburn and skin cancer. Above ultraviolet light are X-rays. This radiation has wavelengths that are short enough to pass through the body or other solid objects. One of the most important uses of X-rays is to take pictures of the insides of the body. The radiation with the shortest wavelengths is called gamma rays. These are produced by radioactive elements such as plutonium and uranium.

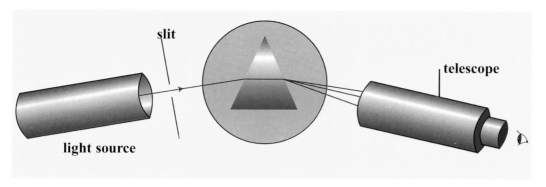

A spectrometer uses a slit to produce a thin beam of light. The light is then split into a spectrum of different colors, or wavelengths, using a block of glass called a prism. The spectrum produced is magnified using a telescope.

The colors a person's eyes detect are produced by different wavelengths of visible light. Visible light with a long wavelength is seen as red. Violet light has the shortest wavelength. This is where the names *infrared* (meaning "below red") and *ultraviolet* (meaning "above violet") come from. Green and yellow light have medium-sized wavelengths.

A source of radiation, such as a star, does not always produce a complete spectrum. Most of the time, certain wavelengths are missing. Other sources produce only a few wavelengths of visible light or other types of electromagnetic radiation.

Uses of spectroscopy

Spectroscopy is the study of spectra. This is done using instruments called spectrographs. Scientists have discovered that certain wavelengths are produced by certain substances. Spectroscopy can therefore be used to identify substances by looking at the light they produce.

This is important in research and industry, where a spectrometer is used to determine the composition of an unknown substance. Astronomers use spectrographs, too, to study the light emitted by stars in outer space.

Discovering the spectrum

The word *spectrum* was coined by English scientist Isaac Newton (1642–1727). Newton gave the word to the rainbow pattern of colored light he produced by shining a thin beam of sunlight through a triangular block of glass, called a prism.

A prism splits white light into different colors by a process called refraction. Refraction is a behavior of all waves that causes them to change direction. It is produced when light passes from one medium, such as air, into another, such as glass. This causes the light waves to slow down. Because some of the wave begins to slow down before the rest, the beam bends (changes direction). Light of different wavelengths changes direction by different amounts. Blue light bends the most; while red light bends the least. As a result, the light forms a spectrum, which can be displayed on a white screen.

During his experiments, Newton saw dark lines in the spectra he produced. He thought, wrongly, that they were intervals between different colors. Many years later, German physicist Joseph von Fraunhofer (1787–1826) discovered hundreds more of these lines.

At first, no one knew how the lines came to be there. Eventually, scientists figured out that the lines were produced because certain wavelengths of radiation were missing. They realized that these wavelengths had been absorbed by gases in the Sun's atmosphere. (Black is not a color. It is produced when there is no light at all.)

In 1859, German physicists Gustav Kirchhoff (1824–1887) and Robert Bunsen (1811–1899) discovered a method of analyzing chemicals using spectra. When a sample of a substance turns into a gas (vaporizes), it produces a pattern of black lines. This pattern can be used to identify the elements that make up the substance.

Spectrum theory

In 1900, German physicist Max Planck (1858–1947) put forward a quantum theory. His idea was that energy does not come in a continuous stream, but in separate packages called quanta (*singular,*

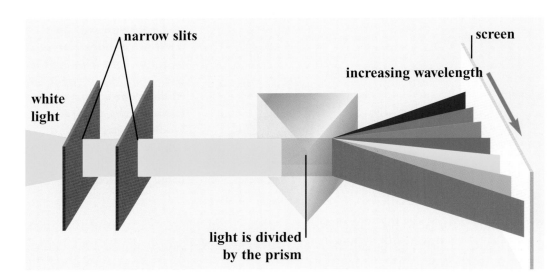

narrow slits

white
light

screen

increasing wavelength

light is divided
by the prism

◁ *Atoms produce radiation at certain wavelengths when they are excited. A spectrometer divides up the radiation into separate beams of each wavelength. This produces lines of light on a screen. Scientists can use the pattern of lines to figure out which atoms produced the radiation.*

quantum). At the same time, other scientists began to build up a picture of how atoms are structured and how they produce radiation. Among other things, scientists discovered that atoms consist of dense nuclei (*singular,* nucleus) at their centers. The nucleus is surrounded by tiny particles called electrons. The electrons are positioned in a series of layers, or energy levels, and they can jump from one layer to another. This new understanding revolutionized the study of spectroscopy.

When an atom absorbs radiation, the energy it receives makes an electron jump up to a higher energy level farther away from the nucleus. When the electron drops down to a lower energy level again, it releases a pulse of radiation. The type of radiation produced depends on the amount of energy the atom is releasing. Short-wave radiation contains more energy than long-wave radiation.

Absorption and emission

The atoms of an element have a unique size. This has an effect on the amount of energy it takes to move electrons between different energy levels. Therefore, the atoms of an element will absorb a unique set of wavelengths. The energy in the radiation at those wavelengths is just enough to move an electron to a higher energy level.

Because the atom has absorbed the radiation, it is not detected by the spectrograph. Instead, a black line appears. The set of absorbed wavelengths is known as the element's absorption spectrum.

Atoms that have absorbed radiation will eventually release it again. The amount of energy they release, and therefore the wavelength of the radiation produced, depends on what energy levels the electron moves between.

When an electron moves from an energy level far away from the nucleus to an energy level very close to the nucleus, a large amount of energy is released, and short-wave radiation is produced. If the difference between the energy levels is small, long-wave radiation is produced.

As with the absorption spectrum, the exact wavelengths released depend on the size of the atom. The set of wavelengths emitted by an element is called its emission spectrum. Heating a gas supplies the atom with energy, and this energy is released as light and other forms of radiation, resulting in the emission spectrum for that element.

Fuzzy results

Atoms that are well separated in space produce emission and absorption spectra that consist of distinct lines. Under more concentrated conditions, when the atoms collide frequently, the lines become less distinct. Under extremely dense conditions, when atoms collide all the time, as they do on the surface of the Sun (the photosphere), a continuous spectrum is produced.

Spectra are also more complex when the atoms have combined to form molecules. Molecules are combinations of at least two atoms of the same or

◀ A scientist studies an absorption spectrum. As well as releasing certain wavelengths, atoms also absorb radiation. This is their absorption spectrum. Scientists can see which wavelengths have been absorbed because black lines appear where the radiation should be in the spectrum.

the angstrom (Å). There are 10 Å in 1 nanometer. The angstrom is named for Swedish physicist Anders Jonas Ångström (1814–1874), who was a pioneer of spectroscopy.

Instruments and detectors

There are four types of instruments used in spectroscopy: the spectroscope, the spectrograph, the spectrometer, and the spectrophotometer.

A spectroscope is used to study spectra by sight. A spectrograph records an image of each spectra, either by photography or by computer. A spectrometer is used to examine a particular group of wavelengths. A spectrophotometer compares parts of the spectrum, measuring the intensity (strength) of the wavelengths present in the spectrum.

Spectroscopes are mainly used by students as a learning aid. Spectrometers are important tools in industry, where they are used to identify unknown substances or check for impurities. Spectrographs and spectrophotometers are mainly research tools. For example, spectrographs are commonly used by astronomical satellites and space probes.

Design and function

Spectroscopes have changed very little since the eighteenth century. White light is passed through a collimator. This is a slit and a lens that focus the light into a narrow beam. The beam of light is then separated by a prism to create a spectrum. The spectrum is often too small to observe with the naked eye, so a small telescope is used instead.

The first spectrographs used a camera to make a permanent record of the spectra produced by different substances The negative image was converted into a graph using a densitometer. This device measured the darkness of the image. Any dark lines left by absorbed wavelengths appeared as white lines on the negative photograph.

different elements, which are held together by a chemical bond. Because electrons are involved in chemical bonding, the energy levels in molecules are different than those in the original atoms. In addition, molecules exist in distinct rotational and vibrational energy levels, so each electron jump involves a possible change in rotational or vibration state. Each transition then becomes a band of transitions—actually large groups of transitions that can only be separated at low pressures. Spectroscopy helps scientists identify the different compounds present in an unknown substance, and it also helps them understand how the atoms within that substance are organized.

Tiny measurements

Spectroscopy involves measuring wavelengths accurately. Although radio waves can have wavelengths of several thousand miles, most of the radiation that is studied in spectroscopy has a wavelength that is so small that conventional units, such as inches, are not useful. For example, yellow light has a wavelength of 550 nanometers. (One nanometer is one-billionth of a meter.) As a result, another unit is used to measure them. This unit is

◄ German telescope manufacturer Joseph von Fraunhofer discovered that the light emitted by stars produced spectra containing black lines in it. Scientists now know that these lines are produced by gases in the atmosphere of stars absorbing certain wavelengths of light. These absorption-spectrum lines are called Fraunhofer lines in honor of the discoverer.

Practical uses

One of the first practical uses of spectroscopy was to check the composition of alloys (mixtures of metals). For example, brass is an alloy of copper and zinc. Knowing the exact amount of copper and zinc in brass is useful for predicting the alloy's strength and other properties.

In the early twentieth century, the spectra produced by vaporizing samples of alloy were photographed, and the results compared by eye. This was not a particularly accurate measure of what was present in the alloy. In the 1930s, the direct spectrometer, which used light-sensitive cells to measure the spectra, was introduced. This produced a more accurate reading on a meter. This invention was important during World War II (1939–1945), when different alloys were needed for armored fighting vehicles, ammunition, and lightweight aircraft.

Alloys are now tested using automatic computer-controlled devices that can detect the wavelengths in a spectrum extremely accurately. Alloys can be tested and approved for use just a few minutes after being made.

Spectrochemical analysis also plays an important part in the fight against crime. Using this method, a forensic scientist can test tiny clues, such as paint flakes on the clothes of a victim of a car accident.

Modern spectrographs do not use cameras and photographic film. Instead, they have light sensitive electronics called charge-coupled devices (CCDs). When light falls on the CCD, the device produces an electrical current, which is used to build an image of the spectrum on a computer.

Spectrometers that are used to detect chemicals do not need to measure the whole range of the spectrum. They are set up to look only for the presence of certain wavelengths.

Photometer is the name given to a device that measures the intensity of light. A spectrophotometer detects the intensity of different areas of a spectrum. Spectrophotometers have many uses. Infrared scanners are commonly used to analyze chemicals. Ultraviolet and visible light spectrophotometers are used to find out how much a material will absorb a fixed wavelength of radiation. Hospitals use this method to measure the amount of dissolved substances in liquids.

In atomic absorption spectrophotometers, a sample is sprayed into a flame. The atoms in the spray absorb energy and create an absorption spectrum. Even tiny amounts can be measured.

Mass spectroscopy

When a sample of matter is bombarded with electrons, it is often fragmented into small, charged pieces. These molecular fragments can be separated by their mass and charge to produce a mass "spectrum." Instead of colored lines, the spectrum is a graph showing the amount of different particles present in the substance. Mass spectroscopy is useful for analyzing complex compounds.

Force fields

Mass spectrometers use electric and magnetic fields to arrange particles of different sizes and charges. A charge is produced when an atom or molecule loses or gains electrons. Electrons have a negative charge, while the nucleus is positive. In atoms, there are enough electrons to cancel out the charge of the nucleus. An atom that has lost an electron becomes a positive ion. An atom that gains an electron becomes a negative ion. Molecules can form ions in the same way.

A vaporized sample is put into a vacuum chamber. (A vacuum is a space devoid of matter.) A typical sample will contain a mixture of different atoms and molecules. Sometimes the sample is bombarded with electrons. This has the effect of ionizing all the particles in the sample. The way a particle ionizes is a useful clue to figuring out what that particle is.

▲ *A chemist prepares a sample for testing in a mass spectrometer. Mass spectrometry uses magnetic and electric fields to measure the mass of particles that make up an atom or compound.*

The sample is then passed through an electric field, which sorts the sample according to charge. Positive particles will be deflected (turned aside) in one direction, and negative particles will be pushed the opposite way. Electrically neutral particles that do not have a charge will not be deflected at all.

Then the beam travels through a magnetic field. This field sorts the particles according to their mass (weight). Smaller particles are deflected by the magnet more than larger ones.

Once the particles have been arranged by charge and mass, they smash into a detector. The first detectors were photographic plates, but sensitive electronic devices are now used.

Atomic structure

Mass spectrometers were used by chemists to help organize the periodic table of chemical elements. This is a way of arranging the elements according to their structure. Mass spectrometers measured the weights of all the known elements. Chemists then used this information to determine the structure of each element.

Mass spectrometers were also used to show that isotopes existed. Isotopes are different versions of atoms of the same element. As well as electrons, atoms also contain larger particles called protons and neutrons. These particles clump together to form the nucleus. Protons are positively charged. Every element has a unique number of protons. For example, hydrogen contains one proton, while uranium has 92 protons. The number of electrons is always equal to the number of protons to balance their electrical charges. However, the number of neutrons (neutral particles) may vary, and this produces isotopes. Isotopes with more neutrons are slightly heavier than those with fewer electrons. Mass spectrometers are used to measure the weight and amount of an element's isotopes.

See also: ATOM AND MOLECULE • ELEMENT, CHEMICAL • INFRARED RADIATION • LIGHT • MASS AND WEIGHT • QUANTUM THEORY • REFLECTION AND REFRACTION • ULTRAVIOLET • X-RAY

Speech

The main way people communicate is through speaking to each other. No other animal has such a complex way of communicating. Speaking is a very complicated skill, and it takes several years to learn how to do it properly. At first, babies can only gurgle, but eventually they learn how to control these sounds to make words.

▲ *Speech therapists help children learn how to speak better. This child is listening to the sounds he makes to help him learn how to turn them into words.*

Talking to each other is the main way that people express ideas and find out about each other. Unlike the other forms of communication used by animals, such as making faces or releasing strong smells, talking is unique. This is because two people can use speech to communicate with each other and express ideas that only exist in their minds.

Sounds and words

Speaking involves using the mouth, lips, and throat to produce a series of sounds. These sounds must be in the right order, so they combine to form words that everyone can understand. It takes hundreds of tiny muscles working exactly right and very fast to form words out of the sounds. This is not easy to learn and takes several years before a child can speak well enough to be understood by everyone.

To make a noise, air must be pumped out of the lungs and up the trachea (windpipe) into the throat. This is controlled by the same muscles that control breathing. Like breathing, this action is done without people having to think about it.

Vibrations in the air

Sounds are vibrations (rhythmic movements) in the air that are detected by the ears. People use vocal cords to make these vibrations in the air inside their throats. These cords hang from side to side across the larynx, or voice box. When they are stretched, the cords vibrate more and produce high-pitched squeaking sounds. When they are relaxed, the sound is a deep hum. The cords are almost completely relaxed for whispering. Pushing more air through the cords makes sounds louder.

Many parts of the body are needed to turn these sounds into words. The lips, tongue, teeth, and palate (roof of the mouth) are used to stop and start the sounds. This produces the "hard" consonant sounds, such as *t* and *d*. The hollow parts of the mouth, nose, and throat are used as echo chambers. These make a person's voice louder and clearer. This principle can be tested by pinching the nose while talking. The voice sounds funny because the echoes have been reduced. People's voices are different because they have different shaped noses and throats. By changing the shape of the echo chambers, especially the mouth and throat, a person can produce the different "soft" vowel sounds, such as *e* and *a*.

When people form vowels during speech, they mostly use the tongue and palate. For example, the tongue is moved up toward the palate and almost divides the mouth chamber into two when the *i* and *e* are sounded. In forming consonants, the lips are used more because consonants are made by blocking the flow of air out of the mouth. For example, the lips are touched together lightly for *m* and opened suddenly for *b* and *p*.

Learning to talk

At first, speech is learned by copying. Sounds and words are repeated by children without an understanding of what they mean. There are several clear stages of learning to speak.

For about the first four months, crying is a baby's only way of getting attention to show hunger or discomfort. Then he or she progresses to gurgling, cooing, and chuckling. At about ten months, the infant starts to repeat sounds, then begins calling an object by its name and asking for something with one word. Around the age of two, most children begin to use sentences. By the age of five, they are using sentences in a more exact way. This is the foundation of speech. After that, a person's speech is developed by increasing the vocabulary—learning the meanings of more words.

Having a conversation

Speech is controlled by the brain. The brain's speech center interprets the words a person hears and figures out a reply. When this reply is ready, motor nerves send messages to a range of muscles, so they can move the mouth, vocal cords, lips, and other parts of the body used in talking. The reply is then made, and the conversation goes on in this way from person to person.

▶ *This diagram shows how sounds are turned into speech. The sounds are produced by the vocal cords, seen enlarged on the left as they make a low-pitched sound (relaxed and open) and a high-pitched sound (stretched and nearly closed). Messages from the brain make the lips, tongue, and palate go into action. Their shape and position alters the sound and creates words out of vowel and consonant sounds.*

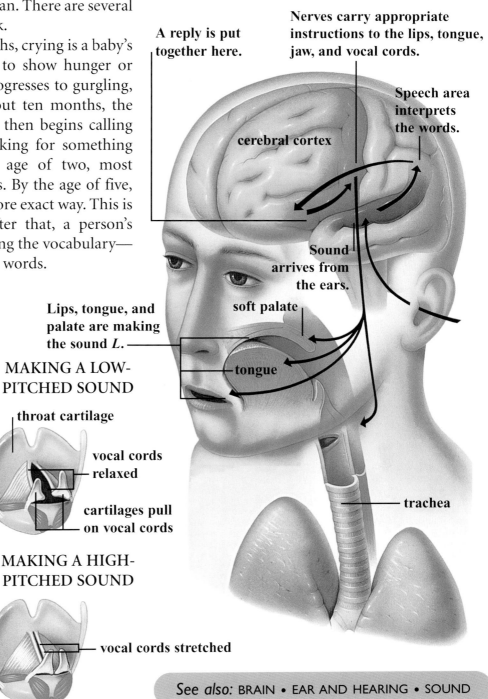

A reply is put together here.

Nerves carry appropriate instructions to the lips, tongue, jaw, and vocal cords.

Speech area interprets the words.

cerebral cortex

Sound arrives from the ears.

soft palate

tongue

trachea

Lips, tongue, and palate are making the sound *L*.

MAKING A LOW-PITCHED SOUND

throat cartilage

vocal cords relaxed

cartilages pull on vocal cords

MAKING A HIGH-PITCHED SOUND

vocal cords stretched

See also: BRAIN • EAR AND HEARING • SOUND

1651

Sports equipment

The world of sports has changed. Modern athletes are professionals, and competition is fierce. Records are broken not only by muscle power, but also by scientific research. As science brings changes, the rule books have to be rewritten.

The equipment that an athlete uses in sports could make the difference between winning and losing. To ensure fair competition, however, it is important that advances in sports equipment are controlled to prevent any competitor from having an unfair advantage. In 1977, for example, the Argentinian tennis ace Guillermo Vilas gave up during a match against the Romanian Ilie Nastase. Vilas left the court because he was getting soundly beaten and could not hit any of his opponent's serves. Nastase was not just a great player, he was also being helped by a new type of racket. Although it was the normal size, shape, and weight, his racket had two sets of strings that were fitted with plastic tubes and woven in a new pattern. The result was that every time a ball was hit, it would shoot off with unreturnable spin. This racket could have destroyed the game of tennis. After the match, the International Tennis Federation banned Nastase's "spaghetti" racket, as it was nicknamed.

▼ *During races, swimmers wear caps and suits that cover most of their bodies. This clothing is made from very smooth rubber. It cuts down the drag force that slows the swimmers as they move through the water.*

▶ *U.S. professional cyclist Lance Armstrong is racing against the clock. His clothes, helmet, and bicycle are all designed to cut through the air without causing too much drag.*

Technology versus tradition

The origins of many popular sports are lost in history. Golf seems to have originated in the fifteenth century. Soccer was initially played with a pig's bladder in the streets of medieval Europe. Any number could play, and there were no rules. Wrestling and athletics were a way of life in ancient Greece, and ball games were played in special courts by people of Native American civilizations. These included a game similar to lacrosse, which was played by members of the Iroquois Confederation.

It was not really until the nineteenth century that sports were organized with rules. The relatively modern sport of baseball formed a National Association in 1858, and the Cincinnati Red Stockings became the first professional club in 1868. Shortly after, American football became popular in universities.

By the 1920s, sports were drawing huge crowds all over the world. The introduction of television brought sports to an even larger audience and resulted in increasing emphasis on professionalism and competition. It became more important to have detailed rules drawn up for each type of sport. It has been these rules that have tended to limit changes in equipment.

There can be no doubt that science is changing the traditional face of sports. Athletes know more about aerodynamics and hydrodynamics (the study of air and water in motion), the capabilities of the human body, and diet. New materials have been developed for making better bats, balls, and protective clothing and equipment. Electronic timing and video replays have eliminated a percentage of human error to make the results of competitions much more accurate.

Advances such as these often make the sports faster, more exciting to watch, and safer to play. However, they not only turn competitions into a race for better athletes, but also for better equipment. Developing new, improved equipment is expensive, so unfortunately today's world-class athletes need money, usually in the form of sponsorship, to be able to compete at the very top.

Tennis: rackets and balls

Until the 1980s, all tennis players, even the world champions, played with wooden rackets. Now tennis players of all abilities use rackets made from carbon fibers that are molded into shape.

Until the 1920s, racket frames were made by steaming a long stick of ash and then bending it into a racket shape. Manufacturers then began to steam and bend several thinner sticks, gluing them together afterward to produce layered frames. In the 1930s, even thinner sticks, called veneers, began to be used. These could be bent cold and glued together with very strong glues. This effectively makes a single piece of wood. Wooden rackets were made largely from ash or beech veneers.

Wooden rackets were strong and light and could bend a little as the player hit the ball. However, as tennis players became better at hitting balls harder, wooden rackets began to break, especially during

▼ *Modern tennis rackets are made from carbon fibers. They allow players to hit the ball very hard. Many people say that the new rackets have made the game boring because the balls now move too fast for players to have a chance of returning big serves.*

serves. An alternative material was required that could make rackets that were as strong and light as wood but could bend as well. Lightweight metals and glass fibers were tried, but by the mid-1980s most professional players were using rackets made from carbon fibers. Carbon fiber is ten times stronger than wood, but it is twice as heavy. The frames made from this material are therefore hollow and filled with lightweight foam.

Carbon-fiber rackets are often described as being made from graphite. However, this is a little misleading. Graphite is a form of carbon used to make pencil leads. Carbon fibers are long, thin strings of graphite. On their own, they are not strong. When glued together, the fibers make tough structures. Often, carbon fibers are combined with other materials, such as metal, to make composite materials with the desired properties.

To make modern tennis rackets, carbon fibers are laid into a racket-shaped mold along with a strong glue called epoxy resin. This resin is also made largely from chains of carbon atoms. The fibers are heated and pressed into a solid shape. This method of production means that rackets can be produced in any shape, and a variety has been developed.

The best place to hit a ball is called the sweet spot. Modern rackets make the sweet spot as large as possible and are more elongated than rackets of the past. For the last 25 years, the maximum size of a tennis racket has been set at 29 inches (73.66 centimeters) long and 12½ inches (31.75 centimeters) wide. The strings can be made from any material, generally plastic, but must be evenly spaced.

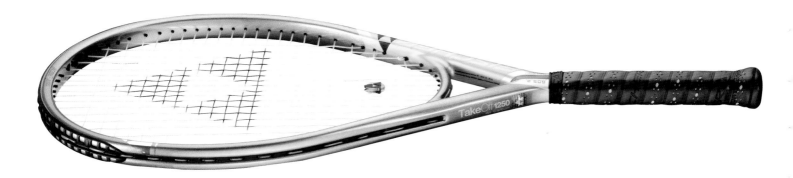

▲ *Tennis balls are made from two halves of rubber that are glued together. The fluffy outer covering is applied to slow the ball down as it flies through the air.*

The original form of tennis was played on an indoor court and is known today as real, royal, or court tennis. The ball was stuffed with soft cloth. The modern game (lawn tennis) started with people playing outside on grass with rubber balls in the 1870s. It was found that covering the balls in felt made them last longer, especially when playing on courts surfaced with harder materials, such as clay. Originally, the ball seams were joined by stitching, but rubber cement is now used instead.

The rubber is now mixed with other materials, including clay and sulfur. The mixture is chopped into plugs, each of which is squeezed into a half-moon shape in a mold. At this stage, the compound is like putty. For it to become elastic, heat is applied in a process called vulcanization. The two halves are then glued together with rubber cement. This hollow core is often pressurized with air or a gas. The outer material is cut into dumbbell shapes, stretched, and glued around the core.

Squash and badminton

The rackets used for squash and badminton have a smaller "face," or hitting area, than tennis rackets. As in tennis, carbon-fiber and plastic rackets have replaced wooden ones; however, the design problems were different. The nature of both games required lighter weight rackets, and the smaller frames and thinner handles needed a high degree of bending ability and extra-strong reinforcement.

Golf: teeing up for the future

Golf is another sport where science has something to offer. Golfers use a set of clubs of different weights, shapes, and sizes to hit the golf ball around the course. The clubs have to meet certain international standards to make them fair. They have always been made with extreme care.

In golf club manufacturing, shafts of steel have been replaced by aluminum or carbon fiber to reduce weight. Carbon fiber produces shafts that are 30 percent lighter, and some of this weight can be transferred to the club head for a faster shot. However, problems remain with carbon-fiber clubs. To make strong shafts, carbon fibers must be lined up along the shaft. This can cause a problem when players twist the club as part of a good shot.

The golf ball would seem to be a simple enough little object, but it too has been at the center of scientific research. It is made by enclosing a mixture of clay, gel, and water in a rubber sphere. A thin elastic thread is stretched around this by a core winder. Two half-moon–shaped shells enclose this bouncy core. They are made of hot, plastic material that has been forced under pressure into cold molds. The finished shells are pressed onto the core under heat, cooled, trimmed, painted, and tested.

The surface dimples are important to a golf ball because they affect how far it travels through the air. When properly hit, a golf ball develops a backspin—as it travels forward, it spins in the opposite direction. This changes the air pressure over and under the ball, causing it to lift. The dimple pattern controls the degree of this lift, as well as reducing the drag (a force that holds it back) on a ball moving through the air.

Athletics: the race for perfection

Running, jumping, and throwing must be among the oldest sports in the world. At one time, the very survival of human beings depended on such skills.

▼ *Track athletes run in shoes known as spikes. In the past, running tracks were made of sand, and runner's shoes had small metal spikes, which gripped the loose track. Tracks are harder now, and running shoes have rubber bumps on the soles.*

▶ *Different baseball players use a range of equipment. The catcher wears a helmet, face guard, and body pads, which protect against being hit by balls pitched at high speeds. The catcher uses a mitt, and the fielders use gloves to protect their hands when catching the ball.*

This may no longer be true, but people still devote themselves to breaking athletic records, and they keep getting faster, stronger, and better. For example, fifty years ago it seemed incredible that a person could run one mile (1.6 kilometers) in fewer than four minutes. Now a four-minute mile is not as great a feat, as many athletes run 10 percent faster than they did in the past.

Part of the improvement has come from dedicated training from an early age and from keeping at a peak of fitness. However, much of the good work can be credited to advances in the design of sports equipment for athletes.

In track running, every second counts. Body sensors and computers are used to model the way a runner moves. This helps coaches to develop an athlete's technique and make it more efficient.

Balls and aerodynamics

It may seem a long way from a physics laboratory to the baseball field, but if a scientist were asked to explain how to pitch a baseball properly, he or she would only be describing what a baseball pitcher does naturally. How is it possible for a pitcher to hurl a ball in such a way that the batter has difficulty hitting it? Baseball pitchers and other athletes who throw or kick balls win games by making the ball curve through the air in an unpredictable way.

Just how a ball travels through the air has been tested by putting it in a wind tunnel, just as one might test the design of an airplane. Smoke patterns reveal patterns of air currents and eddies.

From this, athletes have learned several lessons. The faster the air is traveling, the lower the pressure it creates on the ball. In flight, the air is slowest and the pressure highest at the front center of the ball. Where the air is forced around the top and bottom of the ball, the slipstream is fast, and the pressure on the ball is at a minimum.

As far as physics is concerned, air is a sticky fluid. The friction between the ball's surface and the sticky air causes a small drag. More importantly, as far as the pitcher is concerned, the air forms a layer around the ball, which is carried along during its flight. This air moves slowly over the surface of the ball and is known as a boundary layer.

At slow speeds, the boundary layer remains smooth, steady, and regular. When the ball is traveling at high speed, however, or when the

boundary layer is disturbed by an obstruction on the ball's surface, such as the stitching, it becomes turbulent—it forms whirls and eddies. The action of the seam is therefore crucial to the control of the pitcher over the ball.

The baseball's dumbbell-shaped cover sections are joined by 216 stitches that dramatically affect the ball's flight. One aim of a baseball pitcher is to curve the ball downward to miss the bat's 9-inch (23-centimeter) tip. When thrown into a topspin—forward roll—the stitches drag air around with the ball. The air flow splits and squashes beneath the ball, creating a low-pressure area. The area of higher pressure above the ball pushes down on it, and the ball moves down. A major-league pitcher can curve the ball as much as 17½ inches (44.5 centimeters) on its way to the homeplate.

Safety first

If 210 pounds (95 kilograms) of flesh and muscle come hurtling toward you at a speed of 22 miles (35 kilometers) per hour, the natural reaction is to

▲ *Football players wear helmets and padding to protect their heads and bodies during high-speed collisions during games.*

get out of the way. However, to a football player, collisions are all part of the game. Over the years, a whole range of equipment has been developed for protecting the body. For example, face masks protect the face and eyes, and helmets protect the head. Every part of the body is cushioned by protective equipment in some way.

Ice hockey is another sport that has come to rely on protective clothing. Pads and helmets protect players from flying pucks, razor-sharp skates, being hit by sticks, and collisions with opponents.

In more dangerous sports, science has also come to the aid of competitors. For example, fireproof suits protect race car drivers during explosions caused by damaged engines.

See also: AERODYNAMICS • PHYSICS • POLYMERIZATION • RUBBER • SPORTS SCIENCE

Sports science

Sports is taken very seriously by professional and amateur athletes alike. This also includes disabled athletes, who take part in all branches of sports. Sports science deals with all aspects of an athlete's performance, from sports equipment and training to nutrition and psychology.

Most professional athletes undergo tests at a sports science laboratory, where their performance is monitored while they exercise on a treadmill or cycling machine. Measurements of the heart and lungs are taken during exercise to assess fitness levels and identify problems. However, many sports enthusiasts and amateur athletes are also turning to sports science to help improve their performance.

Heart rate measurements

Measuring the heart rate, or pulse (number of heart beats per minute), during exercise is one of the most important factors in achieving full potential in almost every aerobic sport. Exercising within the optimum heart rate zone is vital because an athlete does not want to stress his or her heart by training too hard. There are many ways to measure the optimum heart rate zone during exercise, but one of the most effective uses the Karvonen formula.

The Karvonen formula involves a few simple calculations. First, the athlete takes his or her resting heart rate just after waking up in the morning. The pulse is taken three mornings in a row. The athlete's average resting heart rate is calculated by adding each pulse measurement and dividing the result by three.

Next, the maximum heart rate is required. The Karvonen formula states that the maximum heart rate is equal to 220 minus the age of the athlete.

◀ Sports physiotherapy is used to diagnose, prevent, and treat sports-related injuries. Working closely with coaches and sports scientists, the sports physiotherapist can increase flexibility, muscle control, and strength; can enhance technique and performance; and can help an athlete return to sports after injury.

Therefore, the maximum heart rate for a 22-year-old athlete would be 198. Finally, the intensity level at which the athlete should exercise is determined. In general, people should exercise between 50 and 85 percent of the heart rate reserve. (The heart rate reserve is a measure of the capacity for an athlete to do exercise above his or her resting heart rate.) An individual's level of fitness determines exactly how far he or she can push the intensity level. A person with a low fitness level should exercise between 50 and 60 percent of the heart rate reserve, someone with an average fitness level should exercise from between 60 and 70 percent of the heart rate reserve, and a very fit athlete may exercise between 75 and 85 percent of the heart rate reserve.

To determine the ideal heart rate zone during exercise, all the information is pulled together using the second part of the Karvonen formula:

training heart rate = (maximum heart rate – resting heart rate) × intensity + resting heart rate

Take a 33-year-old woman who has a resting heart rate of 75. The woman is new to sport, so her intensity level should fall between 50 and 60 percent of the heart rate reserve. Her maximum heart rate is 220 minus 33, or 187.

Using the second part of the Karvonen formula, the minimum heart rate at which the woman should exercise is:

(187 – 75) × 50 percent + 75 = 131 beats/minute

The maximum heart rate at which the woman should exercise is:

(187 – 75) × 60 percent + 75 = 142 beats/minute

As the woman's fitness increases, she can use the Karvonen formula to calculate her ideal heart rate zone when exercising at increased intensity levels.

▶ *An athlete undergoes a VO2 max test to determine her maximum oxygen uptake during exercise. Sports scientists consider the VO2 max test to be one of the best measures of aerobic fitness.*

Heart rate monitors

Ideally, an athlete should measure his or her pulse during exercise to ensure he or she is training within the optimum heart rate zone. The pulse can be taken by hand, but many athletes now use heart rate monitors, which record the heart rate using an electronic sensor worn around the chest. The readings are given on a liquid crystal display worn around the wrist, similar to a wristwatch. In addition to measuring the heart rate, modern heart rate monitors have additional features, such as a stopwatch, calories consumed, and time in ideal heart rate zone. The most advanced models allow the user to download the data into a computer for analysis after the workout.

VO2 max

Most aerobic sports, such as cycling, running, and swimming, rely on how much oxygen the lungs can deliver to the muscles. Sports scientists measure the

this delivery and use of oxygen, calling it the maximum oxygen uptake, or VO2 max. VO2 max is the maximum volume of oxygen a person can use in one minute per kilogram of body weight. People who are very fit have higher VO2 max values and can exercise harder than people who are less fit. An average value of VO2 max for male athletes is about 3.5 liters per minute, and for female athletes it is about 2.7 liters per minute. However, studies have shown that people can increase their VO2 max by exercising between 65 and 85 percent of the maximum heart rate for at least 20 minutes, three to five times a week.

Sports nutrition

Everyone must eat a balanced diet to stay healthy, but it is especially important for people who engage in sports. Before an endurance event, such as a marathon or triathlon, for example, athletes need to eat plenty of carbohydrates. It is also extremely important to consume carbohydrates and stay hydrated during long periods of exercise. Isotonic sports drinks are an ideal solution because they are designed to replace the fluids that are lost through sweating, as well as to provide a boost of carbohydrates during exercise.

Young athletes need special attention. During adolescence, when the body is growing and developing rapidly, athletes need to consume more nutrients than their body size would suggest. Calcium is particularly important. Female athletes may need to include iron-rich food in their diets. Studies have shown that perhaps eight out of ten female runners may be anemic or suffer from lack of iron in their diet.

Sports psychology

Because different people react to stress in different ways, sports psychology is an important part of any training program. The aim is to help athletes enjoy training and to display the right amounts of aggression and concentration during races. They also have to be able to cope with failure and success.

Sometimes even a top athlete loses performance for no obvious reason. This happens because they have failed to adapt to the training load or have been training too much. Varying the training can cut down the fatigue, which often leads to an unexplained loss in performance.

See also: NUTRITION • SPORTS EQUIPMENT

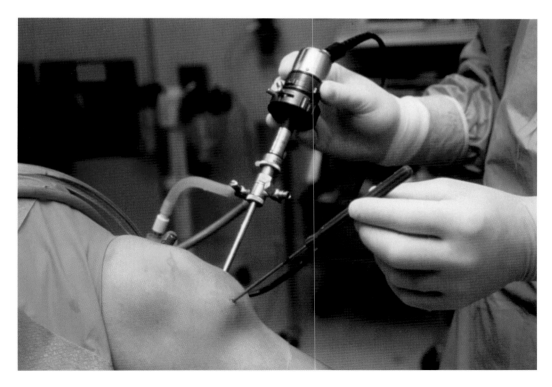

◄ *An athlete undergoes keyhole surgery to repair damaged ligaments in the knee. Sports psychology can help overcome the frustration athletes often feel when they are unable to exercise through injury.*

Glossary

Amplification Increasing the strength of an electrical current by applying a low, alternating voltage to one or a series of electron tubes or transistors.

Asteroid Small rocky body that orbits the Sun between Mars and Jupiter and forms what is known as the asteroid belt.

Comet Small body of ice and dust in orbit around the Sun. As a comet passes near the Sun, a long glowing tail may form as dust particles and ionized gases trail behind it.

Corrosion The breakdown in metals caused by oxidation or chemical action.

Density Quantity representing the mass of a substance, distribution of a quantity, or the number of individuals per unit of volume, area, or length.

Diffuse For particles in liquids and gases to move from areas of high concentration to areas of lower concentration so that the particles become more evenly distributed.

Displacement The weight or volume of a fluid pushed aside by a floating body (used as a measurement of the weight or bulk of ships), or the distance moved by a particle or body in a specific direction.

Distillation Process involving the conversion of a liquid into vapor and then condensing it back to liquid form. Distillation is used to refine and separate mixtures of different liquids.

Electrolysis The process by which the passage of an electrical current through a solution or a molten ionic compound brings about a chemical change.

Electrostatic field An electrical force surrounding objects that have a static (unmoving) electrical charge.

Emulsion A mixture of two or more liquids in which one liquid is present as droplets of microscopic size distributed throughout the other.

Fermentation Anerobic (without oxygen) breakdown of organic substances, usually sugars or fats, to give simpler organic products.

Friction The resistance encountered when one body is moved in contact with another.

Gyroscope A mechanical device with a rapidly rotating wheel that stays pointing in the same direction in space even if its support frame is moved.

Hertz Unit of frequency, abbreviated Hz. The number of hertz equals the number of cycles per second. Hertz are most often used to express electrical current alternations, electromagnetic waves (such as light), and sound.

Integrated circuit An assembly of microscopic electronic components built as a single unit with no connecting wires.

Ionic A compound formed by the electrostatic attraction between oppositely charged ions.

Isotope Any of two or more forms of a chemical element with the same atomic number but different atomic masses.

Metabolism Simultaneous and interrelated chemical reactions taking place in a cell at any one time.

Microorganism An organism, such as a bacterium, that is too small to be seen with the naked eye.

Oscillator An electronic device that produces alternating electrical current. Oscillators are often stabilized using the vibrations of a piezoelectric crystal, usually quartz.

Oxidize To add oxygen to, or remove hydrogen or one or more electrons from, a substance during a reaction.

Permeable The property of a material that allows a liquid to pass through it.

Pitch In music, the position of one single sound in the overall sound range. Sounds are higher or lower in pitch according to the frequency of vibration of the sound waves producing them.

Radiological dating Method of determining the age of a substance or object by comparing the ratios of a radioactive isotope with that of a stable isotope formed by the decay of the radioactive version.

Solvent A substance that breaks down or dissolves another substance.

Vaporize To change in physical state from a liquid to a gas, through heating and/or a reduction in pressure.

Index

Page numbers in **bold** refer to main articles; those in *italics* refer to illustrations.

Index